Hardboot

Books by Vivian Shipley

Poems out of Harlan County (1989)
Devil's Lane (1996)
Crazy Quilt (1999)
Fair Haven (2000)
When There Is No Shore (2002)
Gleanings: Old Poems, New Poems (2003)

Chapbooks

Jack Tales (1982)
How Many Stones? (1998)
Echo & Anger, Still (1999)
Down of Hawk (2001)
Fishing Poems (2001)

November 8. 2006

Hardboot

*for Adele
who is a British kindred soul*

Vivian Shipley

POEMS NEW & OLD

by VIVIAN SHIPLEY

THE LOUISIANA LITERATURE PRESS
SOUTHEASTERN LOUISIANA UNIVERSITY
HAMMOND, LOUISIANA

ISBN 0-945083-13-0 (cloth); 0-945083-12-2 (paper).

Requests for permission to reproduce material from this work should be sent to Permissions, Louisiana Literature Press, SLU-10792, Southeastern Louisiana University, Hammond, LA 70402.

Cover design: Kathleen Tracy and Louisiana Literature Press
Cover images: *The Shipley barn in Howe Valley, Kentucky*, photograph by Todd
   Jokl (front); *The author's grandfather, Charles Shipley, in front of the barn* (back).
Author photograph: Joy Bush
Interior design: Patricia Festa Barnett

  This project is supported in part by the National Endowment for the Arts, which believes that a great nation deserves great art.

Library of Congress Cataloging-in-Publication Data

Shipley, Vivian, 1943-
  Hardboot : poems new & old / by Vivian Shipley.
    p. cm.
  ISBN 0-945083-13-0 (hardcover) — ISBN 0-945083-12-2 (pbk.)
  I. Title.

PS3569.H52H37 2005
811'.54—dc22   2005008702

for my sons

Eric Charles Jokl
Todd Shipley Jokl
Matthew Taber Jokl

and my grandson

Eric Raymond Jokl

⚞ CONTENTS ⚟

3. Hardboot

4. Debris

5. Last Light

1

Act V, Scene iii

WHILE WAITING FOR A BLIZZARD

I have salt, sand, an extra shovel,
a gallon of milk, both cars gassed up.
You get the picture. I'm a safety pin,
belt, and suspenders type. School is
cancelled, so are planes. Marooned,
a time out, some make love, take walks,
but not me. Sleet changes to rain
and I can't enjoy rivers overflowing
from gutters filled with leaves. Snow
does not fall. Instead, robins come,
hundreds of them eating berries
from my holly tree. No weathermen,
their red breasts forecast: spring. So,
why don't I double stock picnic baskets,
buy extra shears to cut tulips, daffodils?

THIS IS BLUEGRASS COUNTRY

On land that had never been an Iroquois battleground,
we didn't even bother poking around for arrowheads,

but there was a story I recited for you about the path
we walked on. Farmers who owned fields on either side

couldn't agree on a common property line. For economy,
each had built a creosote fence to leave a passage

called Devil's Lane. I read lines to you from Robert Frost's
Home Burial about boundaries: *Two that don't love*

can't live together without them. / But two that do can't live
together with them. Standing between pastures freshly

mown, grass green as our uncoached kisses, my arms
were bare to a heat that predicted lightning. Should it strike,

you reminded me, don't cower under a tree. Go stand right
out in the open. Leaning on a post, you compared our love

to gauge blocks, machine shop measures that did not
need anything except their trueness to keep them together.

That day, there were no shapes for words we would carve
to spit at each other, to spray out into our graffiti on a wall.

Hardening as it dried, we mounted our anger like cardboard
pieces of the African puzzle you glued on a mat for framing.

SURVIVORS HAVE VICTIMS

We turn from what destroys us, in time if we can,
and gather what can be held: my grandmother's plate
of full-blown yellow and pink roses scalloped in gold.

Coming back to take what was left of my mother's cherry
chest after the tornado outside Somerset, we found drawers
strewn on the foundation as if a thief, finding no money

or jewelry, was goaded to anger. Devil's Lane was where
we walked that summer my grandfather's farm was leveled,
the cows sucked out as barns flew apart, boards lifting

like souls going to heaven in Raphael's *Transfiguration.*
Clover, there was clover everywhere we stepped. I tied stem
to flower to double wreath my wrist, which had no tattooed

numbers you could recite from your father's arm. Comparing
our love to Kentucky's Natural Bridge we crossed the day
after our wedding, you predicted we would leapfrog old laws

that forbid the marriage of Gentile and Jew. Picturing gloves
made from baby skin in an Israeli museum, you translated
Buchenwald and Belsen into medical grand rounds for me:

experimenting with labor, feet of women were not raised
like a mare's are in a blacksmith's shop, but thighs strapped
together. With no exit, life could not peel from its core.

Strung together, your words couldn't metaphor those mothers,
wombs sealed into a mausoleum. Of course I felt ethical rage,
but there was no common ground in the miles separating us,

Germany to Africa to Kentucky. I mouthed *genocide, holocaust*
to meet the challenge of understanding years I could not pull
myself through. When I saw you holding breath in our shower,

I knew you were testing how long you would last if the water
stopped. In time, there were fences between us that kept rising
like hot air, like the gas none of my family had ever inhaled.

Knowing what cannot be swallowed must be spit out or it will
rot like strings of meat caught between teeth, I choked on soil
planted with your deaths. I couldn't blanket your grandparents'

shadows, could not pull three sons away in time from our flames.
When they smoldered, you fanned them, needing to keep anger
burning, burning through years that can never be consumed.

UNNATURAL

Once the valedictorian, now the father, you flinched
as the son you acquired by marrying his mother flapped
the high school stage, earring and sunglasses glinting,
while his name, not the same as yours, melted into another.
The question had become no longer one of class rank
but of a diploma. Moving Eric's Grateful Dead posters
to North Haven, leftovers from the tag sale in Madison,
you gave him the chance to reinvent himself. Four years
taken from your life could not be replaced like apples
Eric smashed flinging a basket from the table. With a pillow
over his eyes, was he laughing at you during daily morning
lies you told the assistant principal, notes you wrote
as excuses for the body that would not get out of bed,
explanations you created for holes his fist put in doors?
Your sentences didn't even scrape membranes of his sleep.
Did fighting with you ease anger or did he want younger
brothers to hear him numb you with *fuck this, fuck that?*

Guns N' Roses or Pink Floyd from CDs you had paid for
blasted out of speakers too heavy to be hung from chains
he anchored to the ceiling. Teaching you that it wasn't just
sticks and stones but words that could bruise, Eric would
hurl, *Jagger's old, like you, Dude. Both of you should've
packed it in before thirty, showed some class and pulled
a Cobain.* Guilt had grown stale like water standing in glass.
Too much about injustice, the divorce. Too much bailing
water from a ship, holes left by the father, the natural father,
Eric would never understand. What could you say about him?

Stepfather was the salt he rubbed into your skin each day.
His spit on your face, you learned how unnatural this son,
love could be. Waving his diploma aloft, there was no smile
or thumb's up in your camera's direction. The only sign
he gave was a turning, the way a leaf must to the sun. Grafted,
your new life had not taken. After the graduation, you went
to the Rusty Scupper to celebrate. Instead, making sure
everyone who would listen knew he was not your real son,
Eric punched rocks into water, as if Long Island Sound
were your heart. If the two of you had been on either end
of a boat separated by mist, not biology, Eric knew he would
not need to call your name, but could wait to hear your oars
sloshing. No sextant, there was nothing for you to do but
to hold steady, rowing blind through a fog that might not lift.

FUNGUS-YUM

I am twenty, not fifty in this dream,
and when I get to the Boston Garden
to see the Dead, there is a boy-man
who has set up shop selling hookahs
outside the concert. I walk up to him
to ask what they are and he turns.

It is my son, at least my son's face,
pasted on a long tangled mess of curls.
He tells me I'm pretty; I remind him
of someone, but he can't figure it out.
I pretend I know just what to do,
that the hookah is a water pipe used

to smoke marijuana, grass, stuff, tea,
what I called Mary Jane. He tells me
he's at Yale, and I want to understand
why he has set up shop outside the Garden
selling hookahs. It's the good paper he
had on the T, what a blast it is to light up

in front of everyone; it's how he usually
checks out people selling before a show,
but now people check him out as he checks
them out; it's how the perspective is
completely different; like it's how he totally
loves it. I ask if he needs money for food.

He describes his mother, her phony ideas
of success. I use his language: *wasted, suck,*
dude, fucking A. I ask how much the pipes
are worth, where he got $500 to buy them,
what he will do with them during the show.
To show his faith in society, he'll stash

the hookahs in a hole where a stairway
has broken off. He'll put a bag there,
go to the Grateful Dead concert with me.
It's not going to be as total, as awesome
as the old Renaissance Fair Grounds,
their best show in 1972, but it'll hang.

When *Candyman* comes on, it's Vince.
The boy-man with the face, the body
of my son gets pissed at Jerry during
Broken Arrow, Phil's having the best time
and Jerry is staring at his shoes. Why
can't Jerry look up and see Phil having

the time of his life? *Space* is long
and kicks ass. I reach up trying to touch
the boy-man's face, my son's face, because
in this dream, I am twenty, not old enough
to be his mother. Still, I do not understand
him; I cannot wake up from this dream.

COLOR

Air strikes like steel
down my lungs
        stiffens to breath
        crisp like tearing paper
                or sound of my shoes
                printing into asphalt.

A cardinal poses
brief as blood
        red on white mounds rising
        like Christo's umbrellas in Tokyo
                rice paddies or tissue paper
                breasts, swollen and wet.

Ice is clear like flesh
on bones thin as
        twigs of birch trees
        my three boys planted
                last spring. Black
                as periods, these sons

        punctuate the snow, but my body
        drips no color as I run here.

Act V, Scene iii

Romeo and Juliet, William Shakespeare

Chopsticks straightened, sucking orange sections, I pour our tea
and recall driving through Kentucky. Concrete bridged the road,

black paint dripping, *God lie to us.* Blessing's cookies do. I snap
dough to unthread your fortune: *Things are difficult before they*

are easy. This printed strip won't circle you like a rubber band
contracting around your father. A hook, cancer has snagged

his stomach, and he's trying to die but cannot let go of breath.
You stretched out for your son; clots of snow hung as he drove

off, leaving fish tanks filled with neon tetras, metal speakers
from old battle ships, but no note. Now it's my life that divorce

shovels. My three boys will learn where their father is running
another marathon by watching TV. Sounding like a coach,

I read the last fortune cookie: *You can't swim a river without*
getting wet. Abandoning green tea to suck on our red wine,

we analyze two movies you rented last night at Best Videos
to compare how directors can impact a plot. To show off, I

try to provoke an argument about casting: Castellani's use
of known stars versus Zeffirelli's unknown youths. Puzzling

over the constancy of Romeo and Juliet rather than debating
whether Laurence Harvey's display of passion in the balcony

scene erased the final act in the tomb, you feast on Juliet's eyes, her last moment. You want a love that stays to help you through.

If I Get to Choose: A, B, C, D, None of the Above

I won't pick chemotherapy. I'll pencil in *like my grandmother by evaporation at 101,* pick a final breath that does not arouse me from sleep or one that surprises me right in the middle of stripping an artichoke. I refuse to lie here, to worry if I will

live through another season or even last out this September rain. I thought I had felt every lump, come full circle. Ed, the ends are unhooked by your love. You tell me to picture myself standing, head bared, hanging out of a third-class train window

while I plunge through northern Italy. Instead, I invent our story, watch it unwind on tracks, imagine three boys we might have conceived, trading cards to negotiate: Whitey Ford, Babe Ruth, Sammy Sosa, Mickey Mantle, and Mark McGwire. Toeing

limestone, we would have carried our sons, their cleats, smelled mowed grass, heard crickets *a cappella*. When we finally could speculate, say *cancer,* I told you about steering with one finger in my yellow Porsche at 140 to tempt concrete so my mother

wouldn't ask, *Where did I fail her?* Inside my brain, a tumor was hidden like the diamond from your father's Masonic ring I wear on a chain. When I parted my hair to reveal the scar, I was sure you'd leave, but you spoke of deserts you'd explored:

Sahara, Namib, Rub'al-Khali, Atacama, and Takla Makan. Picturing wild berries in Mojave, sweet on stripped branches, you compared me to flowers in the Sonora, hair like petals, thin but persistent. Afraid, I watch out front windows for you to walk up Autumn Street. Skylights frame the black. I cannot stop imagining death might be opening the door and smiling as you do. No promise has been given, but you'll split and pile wood to let winter know we're ready with gloves unpacked.

SNOW

This weather could make me manic.
Light, thin as an invalid's broth,
is rationed out to be sipped as if there
was no hunger for forsythia gnawing me.
No willow with iced dreadlocks, I'm
like an old fir that will snap after bending
too long. Awake, I suspect there must be
a metaphor buried out there. White birch
with Shelley's promise budding their limbs
If winter comes, can spring be far behind?
are not enough to see me through February.
I can quote poetry, but I don't have a degree
from Yale. With a diploma in my hand
I could have joined Mory's, been an old blue
like my Christmas spruce. Evergreen,
I might have seen this storm coming
and hunkered down, all backbone. Instead,
I need a jug of Kentucky moonshine,
white lightning to jolt my bones, to jazz
the junipers that have stayed stooped
for months. Their curved backs spell April
pruning or even uprooting if I'm not sober.

FOR MY HUSBAND AT SIXTY

husband?

Ed, a spade dangles in your hand when you talk, but you have no faith in spring. Summer may not follow, and there is no point in planting day lilies you might not see burst to bloom. On our afternoon drives to Essex, I point out choke cherry seeds that have worked into igneous crevices. You bristle, then predict they'll sprout only to fodder saws of Connecticut's road crews. We cannot have casual conversation: a gull that begs us for french fries outside of McDonald's brushes the windshield but then lands, unfolding its wings like a sheet being pulled over us to cover our eyes.

For god's sake! Wait until May. Plant petunias, marigolds or line the stonewalls with zinnias we can cut. Walk out in early morning, come back around dusk and each orange, white, and yellow will still be there, safe and tame, a sure thing. Don't forget, with no spirit to hold them during the winter, all their blossoms will break off and we will turn stems into compost.

Eat with your head down, go to work, claim the parking spot with your name, come home. You don't believe in immortality so you won't plant sage or, for that matter, mint for wisdom and thyme for bravery. It's sure too late for lavender's purity and virtue. No rosemary, there is too much to remember: your mother in pink dotted swiss dressed for a Halloween party, your father costumed in the purple flowered dress, before stomach cancer caused him to beg you to release him. Still young, your sister is alive, pouting in the car, as determined to stay the rebel as the day she died from starvation rather than live with MS.

Maybe I should plant statice and globe amaranth to give you eternal light. Getting lost in shadowed rooms cluttered like a library full of Hume and Joyce you'll never read, you finger what you have not done, the Phillip Morris stock you sold to come to Yale, the son and daughter you did not raise. The wild seeds you sowed year after year were no metaphor: riding your Harley over Maine hills with Hank, threatening to jump from the balcony of Long Wharf Theater with Michael, being tossed out of every bar after the Harvard-Yale in Boston, the trips from Rudy's to Archie Moore's, then back again. Hands on the wheel at three o'clock in the morning, straightening out Missouri curves for speed, you crossed over yellow lines, singing out *Baby, I was born to run.* That was right before you shattered your hip, the left one that gives you trouble at night.

The bell of a fishing boat sounding out what has not yet drowned, I want my words to knot in you, lash together a raft so you can leave the shore to look for new ground. This far inland, we don't need to fear being lost at sea or the memory of years we have survived that were soft and deep like pond mud. Sucking at our love, anger and jealousy almost pulled us under.

Here in Connecticut, with New England cold that can stretch out through half a year, October to late March, there's a beauty in withered weeks that withstand snow and ice. What can't be seen mixed into summer's foliage steps to center stage in winter. Life-everlasting, goldenrod, pinweed, and wild grass are far more interesting in February than in late July when their beauty is overshadowed by Casa Blanca lilies and the plumes of astilbe. What endures has new strength that can be put to different use.

You'll never be hot pink phlox shedding moldy leaves or an iris whose upright fans can be sheared and reset. Let me compare you to wild yams that blend in with their surroundings in summer. In winter, anyone with an eye for form can't help but notice the three-sided hearts twined in among bleached bones of annuals. Domesticated, plants—even geraniums that are red—do not have your passion or wildness to carry them through the killing frost.

MERRYFIELD

For David Engstrom

I should preface this by saying I do not save ants,
sail them out the back door in a paper towel. Standing
by a stainless steel table waiting to end my dog's life
was the first time I witnessed a death other than ones

I'd caused on a kitchen counter. The mercy was the end
was swift and looked easy. I already had a metaphor:
a poppy's catarrhal rasp spewing death rattle of seeds.
A rose would have pricked Taffy's shaved leg harder

than our vet did. If there was terror, there was no sound,
nerve jumping, nothing. In spite of the face I'd watched
turn white, beauty of red hair over ribs, I dismissed offer
of pet cemetery or ashes to scatter, reasoning the body's

a body, not soul or lantern. Bones cobwebbing liver,
a tumor was the only flesh growing. Taffy would walk
to her dish, look, only to turn away as if the word *water*
was forgotten, but not the thirst. Cubes of beef filet

stayed untouched by her paw. The glory of the body was
that it operated even though Taffy would not eat or drink.
Shrinking, my dog did not turn into something else.
A golden retriever, she dug holes where she could retch.

On her last morning, taking advantage of an open door,
Taffy escaped, hid under junipers while I searched
the yard to leash her for death, knowing it was not
my world, but my dog's that wouldn't return or continue.

A Daughter's a Daughter
All of Her Life

Stirring, pines at Morgan Point ease me
into the day of my son's wedding. First light,

swift as thought of God, of Shakespeare's
searching eye of heaven, cannot scour

darkness from my heart that seizes into a claw.
I think of a tree limb that won't bear new cones,

how it will snap, but how as the rupture ages, sap
will blacken, seal the break. By tonight, my son

will have a wife, my mother's chain and locket with
his round baby face will circle her neck. No way

to sandbag my heart, I must learn to bite my tongue,
control my starfish hands. Rooted in needles

they have shed, evergreens fingering my window
are not like me. They've spent their life knowing

when to bow, how to touch earth like an angler
kneeling in the rapids to let her shining trout go.

LOON

The question that he frames in all but words
Is what to make of a diminished thing.
—Robert Frost

Except for watching loons each day, I can't tell you
how I spent the winter. There were hours in each day;

there were thirty days, give or take, in each month.
I can tell you that carrying their heads and long bills

horizontally, loons dive in the saltwater shallows off
Morgan Point to catch fish. Red as snow reflectors,

their eyes are fiery, but not from sipping Bombay gin.
At least their snakelike scaled necks are good

for spearing stony bottoms—wearing turtlenecks,
I hide mine. Needing to feel superior to something,

I laugh at loons who have trouble walking on sand
in the cove because their feet are placed so far back.

Now, I understand. Where are my sons when I want
an arm to steady me? Both of my boys have married

women not a bit like me. I don't know how to begin
being a mother-in-law. Frozen meals I have prepared,

checks, even my sons' favorite Calvin Klein boxer
underwear that I got on sale are politely refused—

they can do it on their own. I no longer have anything,
say car keys, to withhold. With no card but guilt,

I buy grave plots and ask my sons to come and see
how they overlook the Branford marsh. They will not.

I won't risk uncovering their past I have buried in me.
On the holidays when wives visit, knowing I will say

too much, my mouth is a zipper I dare not open.
Once chicks are fledged, loons are mute like me, but

only for half the year. After six months of being quiet,
these birds who are not afraid to disturb the surface have

a lot to say, calling to each other at any time of night
or day. I envy the loon its tremulous wails, eerie yodel

laughter, screams that are counterpoint to my silence.
Do loons fill the air with noise to celebrate a healing

or to signal the beginning of another season of loss?
Are they like my boys who have forgotten childhood

of Star Wars and Planet of the Apes sealed in attic boxes?
The fists of my sons that used to curl my jacket's hem

now remind me of hail, the ice, the stone I hold inside.
I have nothing for the page because my hands are tethered

by the anger I have roped off. Nagging my heart, I must
give it a voice before I can be released, but only so much

can be healed by words. Submerged in winter, I mirror
loon feathers with my shabby gray hair above white roots,

dingy as snow banked by the plow. Come summer, unlike
this bird I watch diving each day who has learned how

to let chicks go and nest anew, unless I get up nerve, go
to a beauty salon, my head will be not be glossy black,

flashing green in the sun. No dapper ivory and ebony
to checkerboard my breasts, I can not finger a major key.

Unwilling to release whole notes I have damned up, I will
not wail like loons, scream or laugh to let out sound just so

I can learn to sing in combination with my sons to create
harmony. All sharps or flats, I have shifted into minor key.

TRICKY, THE MATTER OF
MAKING A MEADOW

If your heart were a meadow, you could seed at will,
    but don't make plans to sit back like you do
        scattering bread for New Haven pigeons.

Watch out for low spots. Like memory, water pools;
    ground remains soggy. Right from the start, old
        prom pictures, Canadian goldenrod, and purple

loosestrife should be uprooted. Aggressive as back seat
    hands on a double date, they're overwhelming
        like matchbook covers, dried roses, straws

from first kisses. Now, a word of caution: a meadow
    pops up where it pleases; transplanting is difficult.
        Natural field flowers are independent, lovers

who have minds of their own. Keep a list of names: oxeye
    daisy, Canadian lily, black-eyed Susan, bee balm,
        coneflower, sneezeweed, sunflowers. Whether

your heart makes the decision or the meadow does,
    maintenance must be scheduled. Mow in autumn
        after natural wildings have sprung up, forming

seed that will fall to rekindle new growth. Ignored,
    a meadow, like the heart, will toughen and harden
        into a woodland you'll have to chainsaw through.

For My First Grandchild

Eric Raymond Jokl
—September 29, 2004

You are spring, bluegrass
and hyacinth rending tight crust,
harrowing earth that had chosen
not to be opened. Your faltering cry,
quivering lower lip undoes me.
Shining, not a nick or scratch
on you, I think rattling bicycle,
unraveled shoelaces, rollerblades
zig zagging my street, you bear hugging
one tree after another, slamming
mailboxes, lurching into traffic.
You will fall. I see it.
I am already tired, knowing it.

[handwritten annotations: "nature", "baby, new life.", "future"]

2

A Verb from the Earth

FRIDAY TEA: OPENING THE MANUSCRIPT VAULT AT THE ELIZABETHAN CLUB, YALE UNIVERSITY

Afraid I will sneeze, I won't touch a First Folio
of Shakespeare offered by Beinecke Library's curator.
Should I explore—as an academic question, of course—

the purity in Elizabethan speech of people confined
to Appalachian cricks and hollers? Leaving Kentucky
for New Haven, I knew my syllables would unwind,

spill to entangle and mark me like a blue ribbon stuck
on the prize pig at a state fair. Trying to forget the lope
of my accent like a pink shawl crocheted by my Aunt Hazel

I deliberately left on a chair, I shortened vowels, pulling
at imaginary strings with my tongue, extended diphthongs
with a tuck of my jawbone. Still, like signals from men

trapped in Harlan County mines, there were words clawing
in me. In the club library, I watch a man drink Earl Grey tea,
his little finger a comma, and I think of my Uncle Paul,

with a soft rag of voice but no nobleman's British accent,
who was so polite he held a cup to his lips to catch
tobacco juice instead of spitting. I want to hear the hillbilly

in my voice, reclaim parcels of my life that I needed
to keep tied. A real *gosh darn it*, this afternoon I might say
a-sittin' and *a-rockin'* without explaining that the use

of the *a* prefix strictly before verbs ending in *ing* turns
out to be consistent in mountain dialect. As I describe
that *ole woman stumblin' up that there hill with a poke*

and a pig walkin' right beside her, my father saying, *let me
ride behind you on that,* meaning save me the sure bet,
all the members surely will circle me in the garden to hear

a fur piece
no ready mades
a handed-down story
young'uns
tomorry at sunrise.

If I don't lose my audience while reading my new poem
about our outhouse, using an old Sears Roebuck catalogue
for toilet paper, maybe just one Lizzy will cry out

Forever more!

Very Southern
"hilbilly"

WALKING BY 107 WATER STREET
WHERE JAMES MERRILL LIVED

What is the point
if light at Sandover's end
is gone, clams are shut,
tide is out? Rocks of the jetty
might still be hot, slick,
but in the dark, what good
are Connecticut Yankee birds
on stalk legs? In wet aprons
of the bay, James, even marshes
of salt hay, like your poems,
impervious to heat, cold, rain,
snow, offer me no comfort.
What good is crush of white shell,
pink, red geranium window box,
the copper beech on the green
of Stonington, with you gone?

HERE'S LOOKING AT YOU, KID

—Humphrey Bogart
For Leo Connellan (1928-2001)

Heavy, ears sticking out, teeth gone, your jaw was split
by a lover in Greenwich Village. Crossing America,

you laid down first on garage floors to keep your woman
on top, her kidneys from cold. We're not at Rick's Place

in Casablanca but Archie Moore's in New Haven. At the bar
draped in ferns, you try to rise and imitate Humphrey Bogart.

I'm also no Ingrid Bergman, legs crossed on a stool here where
none are strangers, wedged thigh to thigh, elbow to elbow

and so on in silvered reflections. We're in doubt. What's real?
Perhaps what an orthopedist would call spine is looking glass.

Proof is in our touch. If the mirror tilts an inch or two, we'd
have only one eye or Van Gogh's ear. A foot or more, a left

shoulder could be gone. Go further and there would be no
hands to clasp bottles of Jack Daniels doubled by the wall.

If you could be sure when you step out the side door Claude
would shout to his officers, *Round up the usual suspects*

in the morning, you wouldn't worry about avoiding state
troopers by driving back roads of Connecticut to Norwich.

No such ending for you, just seven flights of factory stairs
to sweep for rent. It's early afternoon. Give me your Maine

childhood; recite *Death in Lobster Land;* buy more ale to stop time. We'll never wake up young like those faces on the screen.

COMA: BACHUS HOSPITAL,
NORWICH, CONNECTICUT

I key in *CONNELLAN* on a robot's pad that leads me
to your room in intensive care. You are stiller, older,
and quiet—a phone is not squeezed into your shoulder.

Your daughter puts a hearing aid in your good ear
in spite of the face a nurse makes. My hands rusty,
I pray for words to wing into gulls so you, Poet Laureate

of Connecticut, can laugh with me about the bag of urine
with the brand name *BARD* hooked on your bed.
A doctor says touch and hearing are the last senses to go;

I tunnel a finger, my love, into your hand. Did the stroke
erase running out of gas after our reading at Stone Soup,
hiking Massachusetts Turnpike until the church-going

Baptist took us to the toll station? You thanked him with
a Dixie cup of Wild Turkey. A thief, the clot has bagged
that memory and others: the waiter uncorking champagne

at the Pierre Hotel before your Shelley Memorial Prize,
smoke from fringe of blue jeans Bill Packard set on fire.
The off-season rate in Maine motels with room service

was the makeshift paradise you gave to your wife. If love
of this earth is a way to enter heaven, you will be there,
trying to tear a hole back into this world for fried oysters,

onion rings, lobster dripping in butter. The grandson
of an Irish immigrant who fled to Rockland, Maine, you
were seven when your mother died. Saying she'd gone

to care for another boy who needed her more, your father
took you and your brother to her grave each year, thinking
you'd figure it out. Death will end your childhood dream,

your mother never in it. She will be at the kitchen door
waiting, hands holding muffins studded in blueberries
with names like *rabbiteyes* and *Tifblue*. Leo, go to her now.

A Verb from the Earth

It's not sting of cilantro or the bite of fresh mint but basil
    that makes tomatoes sing. No need for lemon,
    anise, cinnamon, dark opal, or purple ruffle to show
your sophistication, plain old sweet basil will do. History

offers you clues why: tenth-century Chinese cultivated
    it; Hindu gods Krishna and Vishnu regarded
    basil as sacred, and in Greek, *basilikon* meant royal.
Dueling, the emotions of love and hate surrounding

basil since ancient Rome are found in Keats's heroine,
    Isabella, who buried her murdered beloved's head
    in a pot of basil and watered it with her tears.
There are easier ways to grow it. In *To Emilia Viviani,*

the distraught lover received a gift of mignonette and
    sweet basil, *Embleming love and health, which*
    never yet / In the same wreath might be. Would
Shelley have revised this line if Mary had known basil

adds a warm peppery flash to soft macerated berries,
    or that like potatoes, basil is an aphrodisiac? Basil
    is sunny; basil is affable. Tear it by hand. Eat it raw.
Get a little crazy: add garlic, pine nuts, olive oil, Parmesan.

Pound basil in a mortar for your lips that will *O*, sucking
    linguine dripping with pesto. Not just an echo, more
    than herb, basil is bold. Rows may replace high school
bands on Memorial Day. Chop or boil it, you'll overwhelm

your sauces. Its essential oils in microscopic hairlike sacks,
    basil can dissipate like dreams do when exposed to heat,
    heavy knives, or acidity. Words of warning: memory
can be banked in a safe. When ingested, leaves of basil will

be tumblers clicking open the past. Stunning to your senses,
    sweet as honeysuckle or lilac with heart-shaped leaves,
    like love, the smell of basil, the taste of it never had
a thing to do with words, can't be extracted like your teeth.

Cooking with a Dominatrix

I'm a competitor with a weakness for games
that require memory and feel. Contests
with absolutes don't exhilarate me like anarchistic
skirmishes. Actually, I like the duel between good
and evil combined with a challenge that is

altogether tactile. Zesting is one of my favorite
exercises because every lemon, like every man,
is different. I am also a fool for smell. I get off
on knowing I have a powerful, secret ingredient:
lemon rind packed with oil can change even

the odor of my dungeon. The pith, or albedo,
is dense with pectin bitter enough to wreak havoc
on almost any dish, on any client. Only a practiced
hand knows how to lift golden peel from bitter dross,
the exact force needed to tease apart mesh of pain

and pleasure. For zesting, I have no need for chains,
cuffs, collars, and boxes. There's a perfect tool—
one that sports a curved blade. Satisfying as a whip,
there are small indentations on its handle for thumb
and forefinger. The lemon, like a head ready

to be scalped, rests in the palm of my left hand
while my right grasps the peeler and negotiates
between rind and the spongy part beneath. Used
with proper pressure, it produces perfect little
strips of skin that curl through five beveled holes

at its tip. It's not enough for a mistress or her tasks
to control just the body, it is the mind I am after.
Comforting to a man like sucking on a bottle
while wearing a cloth diaper, simple but exacting,
the act of zesting can engender a Zen state of being.

How to Make a Perfect Poem

1. To get rolling, to get in the mood, sing all the verses of Don McLean's *American Pie*. If you lack a voice, inspiration, topic, or metaphor, if like Don McLean, you *Drove your Chevy to the levy but the levy was dry,*

2. knead out balled anger until it thins into compassion by preparing dough for a pie. Never get mad at dough. Treat it gently. Once you understand texture with your hands, the dough will tell you everything you need to know, and like a Ouija board,

3. offer you nuances. What it takes to achieve a tender crust is the opposite of what it takes to make a flaky one. Crisco is the easiest and most reliable, but experiment. Lard crusts, hot-oil crusts, all butter crusts could be like working a word into a poem you have never been able to use, but one you like—say, *tintinnabulation*. Mantra it to soothe yourself while you

4. tighten, while you cut. Like a sestina, it is tricky to create a flaky crust. Combine chunks of very cold fat rapidly with flour because warmth from your hands can melt it too soon. If fat and flour are not flattened, big gobs of melting lard like obvious rhyme will leave holes. Above all,

5. avoid sentiment. Dip into passion. An initial blast of heat will result in an evenly browned rim. Dusting some graham cracker crumbs on the bottom of the pie plate will keep the crust from getting soggy, but allow it to stay tender like a poem should be,

6. considering the human condition. Do not forget generosity of spirit, the importance of largess. There is absolutely no point in putting together a pie, or a villanelle for that matter, if you are going to skimp on the fruit. Who remembers the Home Economist for Swift and Company, Martha Logan, in her Chicago laboratory-kitchen parboiling orange shells to fill with a measly spoonful of cranberry sauce? Live large. Be a Betty Crocker, aim for

7. immortality. When you bake a pie, you pledge allegiance to red, white, and blue gingham aprons, to a straightforward, simple way of life. Cookbook or anthology, bridge two generations, and you will be the one carried from one century to another, tucked right under an arm, all boxed and ready for picnics in Central Park.

An Itinerary for Michael

So alone, you write, *Lord, sometimes, I'm pleased*
this is our only life. It's not as if you need to structure
a sonnet every day, but writing *love* would be harder
for you than chiseling a headstone. My solution?

Head for the armpit of Florida; let your eyes close.
At Cape San Blas, a fishhook of sand snagging
the Gulf of Mexico, we'll drive north on Route 98.
Off the horizon, thin and dark, a line of barrier islands

can become a metaphor for your heart. Keep an eye
out for life, alligators crossing from the right, snakes
or turtles from the left. Smell palm rot, oyster shells,
low tide, shrimp boats. For no good reason, fill up

your mouth with words that don't rhyme: Carrabelle,
Sopchoppy, Panacea, Tallahassee. At Big Bend, air
thick as Jell-O will lure us to walk barefoot, gnats and all,
onto white sand, fine as flour, that my father barreled,

shipped up to Kentucky for square dances in the barn.
If you still feel lonely, Michael, we'll learn the names
of hurricanes: Charley, Frances, Ivan. There will be more
than one story for each of them: houses on one side

of the road, foundations on the other; washing machines
in shallow water that are keeping company with compressors
from air conditioners. For a change of pace, we can turn off
main roads, abandon our car, float down the Wakulla River

where life is the way you want it to be—no surprises
in water so clear, every rock in the riverbed can be seen.
Steering the boat, you may finally get inspired to write a poem
and dare to suggest but not actually include the word *fecund:*

osprey nests, night herons, anhinga drying wings in cypress.
Circling home, if we decide to take the Oyster Route, be ready
to give up control over taste, touch, smell. To bolster confidence,
quote J. Alfred Prufrock: *sawdust restaurants with oyster-shells.*

Be sure to repress, *restless nights in one-night cheap hotels,*
since our first stop is in St. Mark's at Posey's with five kinds
of sauce for pearly gray oysters just tonged up with a wooden
rake from the bay. Even though rubber boots of fishermen are

still whiter than the crackers, Posey's has cleaned up its act,
serves smoked mullet on plastic plates instead of gas-station
blue towels. Pre-historic, the mullet bends plastic forks. Be
a caveman, don't use one! Relax. There will be no need

to wipe your mouth on a sleeve. Napkins are on every table.
If you feel a little macho, dance the two-step, jitterbug, twist,
or Macarena in the hall overlooking the river. Remember there
is no chicken wire to keep you from falling through screens

into the water. After the second dozen oysters, we should
move on to Boss Oyster in Apalachicola. Ignore the roll
of paper towels, and suck or lick your fingers in between
each course of steamed blue crabs, shrimp with heads on,

hand cut onion rings, and barbecue out of the pit. Pitcher
after pitcher of beer will have cups of floating ice. Judge
how sober you are by reading names of shrimp boats: Nixie,
Rosa Marie, Bay Wolf, Marla J. I'll stop workshopping

your senses if you can't pronounce *aphrodisiac* for oyster.
The trip will be complete if you see mermaids lounging
by our table on shells piled into mounds the size of a mall,
if you can hear *the mermaids singing, each to each.*

Upon Receiving a Letter

With my yo-yo, I walk the dog and go clear around
the world, but otherwise, I stand still, look at weed

and bramble. Slitting the envelope, I read that my friend
is taking off for Europe Tuesday, a look at Wimbledon,

a Scandinavian cruise before she begins to study
at Oxford. Her daughters will travel with boyfriends

from Paris to Rome and then explore Italy on their own.
She'll join them for a long weekend in Geneva, then

back to England for a theater course. Imagine, six hours
of credit for going to plays in London with Roger Reese,

Derek Jacobi, and Ben Kingsley! Oh yes, her lecture
at the Folger in Washington went well. It was elegant—

an occasion—one of many she has been allowed to enjoy.
I haven't been anywhere yet, but it's on my list: *let's get*

this act on the road; shake a leg; let's get cracking; I'm
clearing out of here. If I go too fast, I won't see anything.

If I slow down, I won't be here to see everything before
it disappears as the horizon does, a line like black spots

by the sides of my eyes. Turn full faced, they're gone.
At a mosque in Damietta, there is a column of pumice.

If I lick it until my tongue bleeds—it must bleed—I'll be
cured of restlessness. Such choices: spots like my friend's

letter that suck at my eyes or tongues that must bleed. It is
easier to stay put, leave the mail unopened, than to plead:

take me along like floss for your teeth or bifocals you
never wear. I'll be light, no more weight than a paper sack.

Fading like pink liliums, no ardor carries me through July;
everything holds its position: poems, a chair, typewriter

without a ribbon. Perhaps if I could afford to stay on
in Dover when hotels are shutting, umbrellas are folded,

I would decide not to join my friend in London or Paris,
but sit reading in the library next to *Maison Dieu,* or stand

by chalk cliffs that trace the coast. Listening for a gull's call,
waiting to watch light shining on the Strait, there would be

eighteen miles of English Channel for me to cross, opening
like years or the gulf between France, my friend, and me.

The Answer: A Winning Number

You haven't been to Prague, yet?

Gerald Stern, Adam Michnik
Grace Paley, Edward Hirsch
Alan Levy, Vance Bourjaily
Ivan Klima, William Gass.

Shall we go on?

Held at historic Charles University
in July, this workshop is the answer
to your writer's block. Just imagine
lying on your back in a long stretch
of green, a glass of Merlot or—if
you prefer—Perrier cooling at your side.
Watch a white owl circle and dive
from deep blue to lift a gray mouse
clutching a piece of wheat in teeth.
In the face of death, it holds onto life.
This could be just the metaphor, colors,
you have searched for. Roll over, pick
up your Montblanc, position your pad
of parchment on your knees, allow
the heat of your body to rise, to ignite
your words. Ink in another poem.

Give us a call to find out more:
1-800-INSPIRE.

What are you waiting for?

3

Hardboot

WHY AN AGING POET SIGNS UP FOR YET ANOTHER SUMMER POETRY WORKSHOP

I'm inspired by Red Pollard who was also told
he lacked the talent to justify the torture. Red should
have been a poet, not a jockey, pouring over Emerson
and Omar Khayyam. Too tall, he starved himself

until he fainted, put on a rubber suit and buried
himself in fermenting manure piles to sweat off
pounds, swallowed eggs of tapeworms that hatched
to eat the food he squirreled away. Less squeamish

or light enough to race, I would have been called *stereotype*
hardboot, a name given to Kentuckians on tracks
all over the country. Like an old shoe molded
to only one foot, I do have a thick hide that's held up

through years of nettling by tongues of other poets.
Unlike my sonnets, villanelles, Red somersaulted
into history on August 16, 1936, a jockey, down
to twenty-seven cents and a flask of *bow-wow wine*.

Red gave a sugar cube to Seabiscuit, a battered
racehorse, a kindred soul like one I hope to find
on the conference faculty at Wesleyan. Like ham
curing on a hook, my heart still swings from

Connecticut to Kentucky. Writing poems about barns
holding wood shavings from my father's knife,
stains of tobacco he spit on the floor will be like
spitting cherry stones out to breadcrumb my way

home to hills of Howe Valley. In workshops, I will
maintain Red's dignity and smile, not be defeated
by being labeled *easy to read, plain of speech,*
or *ordinary.* Unlike Red, I was not abandoned

at fifteen on a racetrack cut into a Montana hayfield.
There has never been any need for me to thumb
through *Job* to cheer up. Because my feet grounded
in bluegrass generations ago, I'd had my chances,

but never rode bad horses by day or slept in their stalls
by night after getting punched bloody by cow-town
boxers. So, Red would be my subject for the list poem
on the summer syllabus: chest crushed, left eye blinded,

leg almost sheared off, teeth kicked out, back and skull
fractured. Until Seabiscuit's last race—March 2, 1940
at Santa Anita—Red said they *were a couple of old
cripples together, all washed up.* They rode to victory,

drawing a crowd of 78,000. I can picture myself reading
poetry to them. A hardboot like Red, I refuse to believe
my hopes exceed what nature and fate bestowed. There is
always revision, change in literary taste, *The New Yorker.*

For the Unnamed Woman in a Photograph at the New Haven Colony Historical Society

Fixing dinner fit for a preacher, there's no slow syrup
hours on Sunday for you. It's not Pulaski County,
Kentucky, but Fair Haven, Connecticut. Exchange
squirrels, hog feet and brains for your fish and clams,
you'd be my Grandma Todd in an apron trimmed

with rickrack bent over a soapstone sink holding strainer
and knives. Spare time's for fixing. Rocking while a stove
heats to red, your fingers have to be busy shucking raw
oysters in pans set on a square table or turning collars
until pots of water fog the windows. Like my grandpa

who took off for the cow barn before dawn, tomorrow
your husband will be out with first light. Squirming
like an eel out of water, mornings he smells for stench
from low tide before it turns. You'd like to pan fry a mess
of dough for his lunch pail, but all he wants is mackerel

as he storms at you to dock your nonsense, shake
a leg or overtime will be paid to his boat's crew. Sleep
only widens the space between hours that are tweezed
of pleasure, of friends that will not be given back to you
on this earth. If you did not corset days with work,

what would you do? Nets to mend piled by the door keep
you inside. There's no way for you to pull yourself from
the catch your husband takes from the Quinnipiac River,
any more than the lobsters struggling on the mud-caked
linoleum can save themselves from your boiling pan.

Sitting with My Grandmother,
Parealy Stewart Todd

Old stalks bleached from brown and pith dried, your fingers
can't peel or dry apples, hull or crack hickory nuts for jam cake.
Never thinking like Uncle Alonzo of how much tobacco could
fit in the back field, your vegetable garden was ploughed edge

to center, furrow to furrow squaring off as soil darkened under
weight of Snip's and Nellie's feet. That ground Grandpa fertilized
closed slowly, denting like dough you kneaded for the biscuits
I smeared with blackberry preserves scooped from green jars.

All broken now, like windows in your white house emptied
except for a velvet jacket hooked on a parlor door you wore on
your golden anniversary. At my touch, a bat I mistook for cloth
flew to hang on a sill. I would have brought it with me today,

but I was afraid there might be another bat, then another,
bunching like black walnuts with husks splitting for squirrels,
that quivered with hunger as I did at sixteen. Knowing thirst
work would quench, you'd wake me to hoe beans, scatter hens

that seemed to cluck: find a man, get married, have children.
There's nothing more. After Sunday services in Somerset,
I waited for a boy who wanted to take me behind the barn,
tongue my mouth, but you called me back. Frying chicken

came before sin. Grandpa had taught you breaking a mule
was mean business a girl didn't understand, even one like
Betty Grable looking over her shoulder in a white bathing suit.
Lord knows, Ava Gardner had tried. That was the year she met

Mickey Rooney. Mid-afternoon, you gave me the frosting
bowl as if licking brown sugar would fill me. I have crossed
off dirt roads from your map and marked interstates in red.
Why can't I drop your hand, plow you under like seed potato?

o coming of age ~16.
· grandmother-past

White Chickens

The image of a straitjacket has come back to me.
Flat, folded together, sleeves open and reach out
like white wings flapping the backyard my father
fenced trying to update the farm, rein in chickens
that ran, nested in the barns, and laid eggs in hay.
Crowded after hatching, because they were bred
for slaughter, his new batch of fryers never walked.
The optimist, each morning before his coffee, he
positioned them, statues on the grass of two roosters
and thirty hens that had been cooped up too long.
It should have been easy for him to wring their necks.
Was it boyhood need for chase that left him unable
to kill or did my father expect our chickens to twist
off their own heads and plaster grass with their blood?

WITH MY GRANDFATHER TODD THE SUMMER I TURNED SIXTEEN

Take jewelweed, you told me, for the sting
of nettle, digitalis for a broken heart. The bells
of jimson weed were bitter, but pennyroyal
with small lavender flowers spread over

a field was the sweetest of wild mints. Heal
sprains with comfrey, rashes with goldenseal,
burns with aloe. To show me passion, you
compared foxfire, a luminescent fungi even

in decaying wood and leaves, to fifty years
of love for Grandma. Picking blackberries,
you wore black leather fish gutter's gloves
that my father brought you back from Maine.

Because the fingertips were cut out, you could
feel the fruit, soft like a heart, ease it off briars.
The juice, the lard crust of a hot cobbler were
worth pain. No way you knew to keep them

from being born, you took me to the creek
with you to drown kittens where they'd wash
away, making me watch, telling me not to give
life to anything I couldn't feed. Your lesson held

on like moss through the years when I needed it.
You are not here to celebrate tonight, the ninth
of July, to guide your great-grandson, Todd.
As he turns sixteen, I'll give him a circle of gold

you hammered from a coin for me. Your ring
will remind him as it did me that sometimes
in the bad we do, there will be good that can
turn on us as a surprise when we need it most.

gives hope for future.

family | past
Past connected to present

THE FAITHFUL DAUGHTER JUSTIFIES
POEMS ABOUT HER FATHER'S CANCER

My father's a lucky man,
not like those ducks
on Grandpa Taber's pond.
A boat of white feathers, feet
were the first to be gripped
in jaws that had stayed beneath
layers of silt, husbanding survival
by eluding fish hooks. Only a thin
lifeline of bubbles to surface
betrayed the turtle. A burst
of muck air, no picture
or headlined obituary recorded
a death so quiet, a death so small.

PLANT HONESTY, MOONWORT, MONEY PLANT

A spade dangles in my hand as my father and I talk.
He does not have the heart, the bones to work cold
ground when for him, April is not a sure thing. We

try to have a casual conversation about divorce. Unlike
me or my two sisters, swans in the cove mate for life
like my father and mother. So do herring gulls, floating

for fried shrimp tails from Jimmy's in West Haven.
Spreading wings to dry, they are a shroud or muslin used
to wrap his faithful mother. No interest in planting tulip

bulbs that would be a spring inheritance, my father won't
discuss avoiding taxes, setting up trust funds. My eyes
weasel, thin to scratches on a record: grandsons, tuition,

how I sure do wish his parents had left money to let me
show off an Ivy education. Saying I'm not too old to learn
to spout Latin, that *Lunaria annua,* the money plant pods

he gathers, were brought to England in 1595, my father
describes moons flowering, my mother in white satin.
I see four quarters, translucent disks big as silver dollars.

faithed
reminising

MOONFLOWER

Silence wakes me more surely than a scream.
At three in the morning, sound on the baby monitor
is what I listen for: clearing of throat, motor
of hospital bed, flushing of toilet. It's to my father,

to his movement that I am bound. A moonflower,
mouth yawning, arms stretching like petals, he
wakes, slow, sitting on the bed's edge to avoid
vertigo. Sallow skin, cream yellow of moonflowers

whose stems tighten around their minutes of glory,
their minutes of life, my father curls his fingers
around his cane, his pride. Even driving, my mouth
twisted into a handkerchief at a funeral, his death

is what I can't escape. Go to the dentist for a crown,
sure enough, my chair faces tombstones I count
while black plastic bags acrobat the cemetery walk.
Afternoons, asleep in his blue hospital chair, my father

is so still, I stand until I am sure paper whispers of lung
rise and fall in his eggshell chest. When will I layer it
with a tattered shawl of rosebud from Howe Valley?
Bound to motion like the moonflower, there can be

no escape from the rack of this earth for him, for me.
By spring, I may be a supplicant by my father's grave
next to a dogwood with stigmata on white petals
that will fall to pinwheel then cover him in the ground.

STONY CREEK GRANITE

Unexpected, this Connecticut day melting
winter, seasons still locked in the ground.
False Spring, my neighbor calls out to me
as I watch him rebuild our boundary wall,
bind the land with thriftiness of line. The top
is already spilling over into the dirt; flat rocks
bend down as if yearning to avalanche.

Rehearsed in lifting gravity, realizing that
earth does not repent, then cast out stones,
he points out boulders that his numbed hands
will pry. We can see there is no final resting,
that our spring ritual is just like putting out
a leaking pan to catch rainwater for my hair.

Knowing I'm no Robert Frost, my neighbor
is my friend because he takes me, my poetry
seriously. It's my job to watch, to comment,
maybe find a metaphor. Never one to shirk duty,
aware of what I will provoke in him, I offer,
Odd, the tension in unhewn, unmarked stone.

Sure enough, he stops wedging pieces of granite
that are worn to pink, not speckled in gray
like the photograph his uncle took of his father
standing by the base of the Statue of Liberty.
My neighbor never tires of pulling the picture
from his wallet and talking about the statue,
how its foundation is built of our same pink
Stony Creek granite. His grandfather quarried it

in Branford, blasting sections to cut for engineers
with their charts that were fortification against
frost that heaves the earth. Tired out from
all the work, I decide to leave my neighbor here.

In the morning, I'll ask him how he would describe
our wall when muffled in snow or fringed in grass.
Sunset is the good hour for him, spent watching
red-tailed hawks float, never measuring days
in hours taken to tie stalks of corn as my father did.
I used to watch Daddy gaze skyward, appearing
to measure Howe Valley fields out of his reach.
I wonder if, after all, my father was like me, was
looking for stones, for a light to guide him through.

There Were the Signs

Seeking New England's wisdom, I turn to Robert Frost:
I think I know enough of hate / To say that for destruction ice

Is also great. I know, Mother, I could've prepared for this cold
spell if I'd listened to you describing crows gathering, birds

flying low, and thick fur on the bottom of a rabbit's foot. Water
in Morgan Point's cove is iced over. What might be water lilies

crack like skin on Daddy's hands or scales of the Loch Ness
monster. I could be standing by ruins of the Urquhart Castle,

with thunder cutting deep through the mountains of Scotland,
but I'm in Connecticut. Tide comes in with pads of white slush

roping into strings of salted garland on gray water. It should be
Christmas. Snowed in, I'll die in ice unless I regather days of fog

from August to number wintry days of December. I should stop
wasting persimmons by piling them in glass bowls and slice one.

I can hear you repeat, *Read seeds: the shape of a tine spoon means
snow to shovel, a fork, a loose easy new year, and a knife, a sharp*

January. When all else fails, I could try to find a hornet's nest.
High in trees, the snow would lay on; low, don't unpack chains.

Cut off from you back home in Kentucky, Mother, I am not
to blame if I didn't see corn shucks were heavy, hard to take off.

Weather will be fair if the owl screeches, but all I have are gulls.
I could keep flight charts, live with what surrounds me as you

taught me the Papago Indians do. Living with the black widow
and fire ants, they don't step on a rattlesnake spiral or disturb

kit fox bones. If water is scarce, memory makes a fossil of rain
just as ancestors of Papago, the Hohokan, did. Bones under sand

in marine limestone, their history is painted on red clay like you
plowed in Kentucky. Far from Long Island Sound and its snow,

housed by wattle and daub, Hohokan had no need to build with
chinking and logs or trap for furs. From them, Papago learned to

weave fine cotton to keep hot sand off skin. Mother, you taught
me how to live in heat, give my body to wind, but not about ice.

Southern who is naoin north
- could not prepare for cold winter

MY MOTHER'S FACE

I no longer bother to lipstick
my mother's mouth, but I oil skin
to erase creases I have caused.
No verbs in her lines, only a pronoun:
me, the dropout of confirmation class.
Keg parties, broken curfews wore
her beauty away. Alzheimer's
has taken these nouns, but not love
soldiering through to camp in the heart
I did not deserve. Forgiveness,
her last gift to me, could be in furrows
that I smooth above her eyebrows
if the smiles outnumber the frowns.

AND THEY, SINCE THEY WERE NOT
THE ONE DEAD, TURNED TO THEIR AFFAIRS.

—Robert Frost

Shirtsleeves rolled or collar turned up
to Kentucky wind, it's always men who share
coffin weight up Science Hill to where it's flat

enough to dig a grave. The oldest women kinfolk
will have done their job, moving a black rectangle
from border to center of a burying quilt covering

the lid. Sitting with my mother in The Arbors,
I unfold square after square of the heirloom
of darkness our family has passed down

like a pocket watch. On the blue flowered edge,
four coffins remain. I know I am breaking tradition
by unraveling thread before my mother's death,

but sewing is a tourniquet for my nerves, will be
one way to wear down the clock. Suspicious
by nature, living in tomorrow, done with today,

Mother wants to be sure her quilt is ready, directs
me to line her casket up like a used car by graves
of Burnadean and Hazel, her sisters who have gone

to their reward. When I put down my needle, there
will be three scraps to move. I name mine *obsidian*.
Wallowing like Grandpa Todd's gray hog, I wonder

if the two sisters I do not see year-to-year except
when grief or marriage vows unite us on a pew
will move my coffin to center. I've already paid

for eight Connecticut gravesites so my three sons
won't have to climb up Science Hill to level ground.
The family plot I own is above the Branford River.

Tide was out, muck exposed when I chose the land.
Worrying about a view I wouldn't see, I spotted
an osprey's nest in marsh green of summer, wanted

my feet pointing to its perch, not subsidized housing
on the hill. Controlling what I can, I am comforted
by knowing what spot of earth is mine. Will I learn

to accept tide, as the river does? It's not the coming,
water high in cattails, but the going that undertows,
mud flats slicked on sticks like bones of an opossum

I can't resist eyeing on morning walks. As its body
dissolves, the skin blackens to shine like wet earth.
No quilt for the opossum. It's easy to accept a death

that's not Mother's, not mine. What I fear in others
is myself—that I won't pause to mark the morning
I no longer think about pulling my retriever away.

ALICE LEE TODD IN THE LOOKING GLASS

In a Medicare room with a mirror on one side and an object,
say, my mother propped up by pillows, on another, if I face
the mirror, because the walls are close, I can step forward

to my mother's likeness. Reaching back, I can't touch her
kneeling with a Comet can by my bathtub, or dropping wads
of paper towels like a flower girl at a wedding as she washed

my windows. It's easier to look at my mother in a mirror than
to describe what she does to my heart today in The Arbors.
Unable to speak or feed herself pureed food, she can't squeeze

my hand. I remember—cylindrical, spherical, convex, concave,
flat, or wavy—reflected objects retain their spatial relationship,
help keep perspective and distance. I become confused only

if I forget, like that time I won the poetry recitation. I pranced
home, head stuck up prissy as a moccasin swimming on top
of the water. My mother stopped only long enough to twist

her head around from pruning grapevines for wreaths she'd
sell for a *pretty penny* at Berea College. Nothing's changed.
Her bed, my chair are two feet apart but we are not close. Love

isn't simple like congruence of our faces in the mirror. Clean,
it might reflect imperfections or become a channel for unaltered
embodiment: my mother backing into the porch's screen door

with her hip or rubbing her forehead with the heel of a hand
after doing supper dishes. To forget, it would be worth the price
of admission to fun houses with mirrors that distort then conjoin.

I remember us playing Hearts. I would hold up a fan of cards,
allow them to tilt in order to hide my eyes, mask the need
to win approval. Partial copies of her in carnival mirrors would

confuse me with artifacts of the mother I want to create, a past
I need to settle like using place holders to seat guests at dinner.
Square or round, silvered glass fuses our life to cooking lessons

on TV, which loses the smell of scored basil leaves and garlic.
An oval gilt mirror might bring us together by curling around
like a gray cat I yearn to be who is untroubled by union of sight

and smell or impossibility of wholeness. If only my hand were
more than a reflection, I'd reach out, try not to fail my mother
again: the Kentucky Homecoming Queen who was not crowned,

stretching for rhinestones, red roses, straining to hear my name
blaring from stadium speakers so my mother in the stands would
hear, would finally be proud. Could a mirror guide me to just one

night she might have quit working long enough to come, cheer
at my softball game? Summer heat, playing under lights, running
from smell of sewage, I would catch my breath like a grounder

when she sat down in the front bleachers. No. A mirror will not
show me what didn't happen. Unity and completion are needs
mirrors can't fill, only prove the impossibility of feeling sting

of my mother's knees bleeding from carpet burn as she climbed
risers, one by one, to wipe dust from stair corners. My poems,
substituting words for a life that is lived, do not fool anyone

like my mother did, leaving lights on in the chicken coop to get
nesting hens to behave as if it were day. Unlike poems, mirrors
will not interpret or correlate internal and external self, present

experience as a simile. Like helium that seeps from birthday
balloons, words of praise my mother did not give me were not
in her. Work suctioned out the joy. Showing that she cared

by ironing my blouses, my mother didn't have breath to waste
on talk, and I couldn't tell her that I needed her words more
than starched collars. Listening to her snore as she sleeps,

gaping mouth almost emptied of teeth, I learn her final lesson.
It won't be a mirror I wipe sausage gravy from, but her chin.
Without saying it, my mother taught me the word: *love*.

4

Debris

No Deliverance

September 11, 2004

Long, unbroken, heat has driven a raccoon
to mouth water in trays holding philodendron

I have positioned to catch early morning sun.
With no words to share, no sign language,

to communicate, maybe to show my power
over physical need this animal cannot control,

I set out a slaking bowl. All I do is crater
withered grass with white ceramic. Untouched,

the water stands all day as if it held my scent.
Remembering smoke, towers, planes, bodies

in air I'd witnessed mid-morning three years
ago, I twist my hair around a finger as I watch

the feral eyes rimmed in black that punctuate
arborvitae binding my yard. If I could zipper

the scar from a brain tumor that connects scalp
hooding my skull and pull skin down to unmask

sinew, a tame heart beating, I might cut razor
wire fear that keeps this raccoon away, stops it

from assuaging the thirst for life we both share.

DEBRIS

> *"There's an east wind coming, Watson."*
>
> *"I think not, Holmes. It is very warm."*
>
> *"Good old Watson! You are the one fixed point in*
> *a changing age. There's an east wind coming all the*
> *same, such a wind as never blew on England yet. It*
> *will be cold and bitter, Watson, and a good many of*
> *us may wither before its blast."*
>
> —Arthur Conan Doyle from "His Last Bow"

I. BERCHTESGADEN'S PUBLIC SECRET

That's what Florien Beierl calls me. Afraid,
I have signed a lease as Frau Wolf, but, Adolph,
everyone knows I am your sister. Illegitimate,
our father, Alois, had our grandmother's name,
Shicklgruber. Because you used his surname,

Hitler, I did too. Before shooting yourself in Berlin,
you said farewell to Joseph Goebbels and Albert Speer,
but left no word for me. Adolph, why did you close
your heart, shape it into a fist that's become an incubus
pounding in my veins? To the end, Eva Braun,

common shop assistant, was cowardly, took poison.
How could you disgrace our family and marry her
the day before you committed suicide? No concern
for my fate, your death was not an end-stopped line.
I was left adrift, an outcast in two ground floor

rooms near the train station. New tenants upstairs
say it's strange that I do not take refuge in my alias,
lose myself in another town's festivals. I will not

tell them I take comfort being near what remains
of you. Early on in April, the SS abandoned

the Berghof. Neighbors, women I thought were friends,
went with or without wagons, carried what they could.
Not much is left of your house, only door handles,
patio stones someone will soon have in their back yard.
My butcher allows me to lift the receiver of a phone

he yanked out of your bedroom, but the dentist who took
six volumes of your Shakespeare won't let me massage
the swastika or your initials, A.H., on leather spines.
I do not dare tell them I have the four letters you sent
me in 1924 from Landsberg sewn into my mattress.

That fat, swarthy woman who sells eggs denies me
even a snip of your hair, gotten, she says, from the barber
who brags each day that he trimmed the Fuhrer's mustache
even though he knows, as I finally do, how bodies
of children shriveled, how the ash lifted with the smoke,

rising slowly because it was heavy with bone. Yet,
I cannot corral our childhood by stopping memory
of you, my shield in the streets of Linz, or the bonfires
you lit each fall to amuse me. Adolph, stiff as a scarlet
taffeta skirt, my heart still cartwheels if I hear your name.

II. *Please remember he was my brother.*

—Paula Hitler

Brother, it is May 1945; you are dead. George Allen,
United States Army Intelligence, wants to question me.
He knows I am Paula Hitler. I refuse. I must go out

to the bakery. If I am late, dark brown rye will be gone.
The interpreter promises me bread; I have no excuse.
Adolph, shut up in a car with them, pressured to say

something about you, I try *die schonsten Zeiten seines
Lebens*, how you passed the most beautiful time
of your life in the Berghof's ramble of three stories,

balconies, and picture windows. Pitched roofs
intersected like a jigsaw puzzle of our life I never
solved. I hope detail satisfies George Allen: white

armchairs under striped umbrellas on a patio, Eva
holding Goebbels's little girl whose hair was topped
with a white satin bow shaped like the swastika

stitched onto a white patch on your left sleeve.
Finally, George Allen smiles, takes notes as I recall
how you never cared much for meat in our youth.

Our mother gave us cheese, fish, and game fowl,
but no blood sausage, veal, or roasted flesh. Even so,
you buttered toast as if flaying sinew from a bone.

Cheese ravioli would have been one of your final
meals. I picture you cleaning your plate while Eva
picked at the pasta as she lit cigarette after cigarette.

Indifferent to clothes and food, you never smoked,
drank tea, coffee, or alcohol. Hungry, hoping to free
myself from endless interrogation, get loaves of rye,

I uncover the scar, a new moon, your teeth left
on my left arm. No fermata of love, it is a lesson
I do not forget even for fresh bread. Our interpreter,

editing *lower-middle-class woman of great religion*
but no intelligence, does not realize I understand
English. He does translate that I'm a sister *whose*

misfortune it was to be related to a famous person
with whom she had nothing in common. Provoked,
I offer the men what is not mine to give: your tears

at our mother's death. How can this uniformed man
understand that blood we share still pulses in me
like your knee knocking, knocking at the underside

of our kitchen table? My heart has not uncoupled
from my mind, and to stop George Allen, I begin
to sob, show him what he wants so he will not need

the translator. At last, he concludes: *It is clear you*
have been deeply affected by your brother's fate.
I reply, frightened, *By his personal fate, of course.*

III. Paula Hitler's Last Confession

Father Gustaf, you ask what it is I cannot forgive.
My grievance against my brother that I cannot
dilute or dissolve arrows my heart. Memory
is a wave carrying a log from the cove only to

wash it back in a storm. Does forgiveness come
in the telling of a story? If so, let me tell you mine.
Our father died. Adolph was fourteen and failing
in school to defy him. Hanging out with sculptors,

working with wood, he'd learned about the heart,
how it splits like timber down the full length
of the plank. Take a solid piece, drive in a wedge,
give a hard twist, and it will crack end to end. All

my brother needed to learn was where the grain lay.
Unlike our father who never spoke of love, showing
it in his will and life insurance he left, Adolph could
break my heart with a word. Mother's lapdog, clever,

systematic, for three years before her death, Adolph
withdrew small amounts from our father's trust so
the theft would not be noticed. And what could I do
once I knew what had been done—hire a lawyer?

No sum could replace what had been stolen. Dying
of cancer, our mother gathered up strength to sign
an undated lined yellowed page giving my brother
an allowance to live in Vienna. Left with nothing,

I had to forage in Linz. How can I die in peace when
the words *treachery, theft, deceit, cunning* jackhammer

my heart? I suppose there was concern for my safety.
Before leaving, Adolph taught me to break a man's finger

with my teeth—right below the knuckle is easier to grip.
Father, I confess I took pleasure when he was denied
entrance to the Academy of Fine Arts. Painting postcards
and advertisements, my brother shut me out by moving

from one Vienna room to another. Years passed, I sinned
again, cursed when Angela, not even a full sister, came
to live at the Berghof. Her daughter, Geli, killed herself
because of Adolph's jealousy. I spit *blood-kin* in his face,

held up their picture to goad him: Geli stretched beneath
his chair, the bold geometry of her sundress in contrast
to grass, her saddle shoes, white socks. I had never been
given such a look from him. Father, it does not matter

what history makes of me. Invent a life for the press—
I ate persimmons, roasted chestnuts. Report hope I had
for my brother's love still mocked me, a maraca luring
me onto the floor when there was no one left to dance.

IV. FATHER GUSTAF, GIVING LAST RITES TO PAULA HITLER

Unlike your brother who committed the ultimate sin
by taking his own life in Berlin, you will be buried
not burned. If you had been in his bunker, you would

have cried out, *Adolph, you never left the Church.*
Do not leave it now. Wait as I do; let God take you.
Let Him take you to our mother. Paula, you could

have persuaded Magda Goebbels not to take the lives
of her six children by forcing capsules of cyanide
into their mouths while they slept. Our townspeople

do not practice *Sippenhaft,* punishment for the crimes
of blood relations. At the gate of Schonau am Konigsee,
the cemetery director who understands a heart can crowd

out the mind will not admit those who come to desecrate,
only mourners to commemorate, to light a votive candle.
Paula, your brother's already our history. There's no way

to understand the absolute monster he was, to revise evil.
Your family is remembered. Dollensheim's square was
renamed *Alois Hitler Platz* after your father; Spital has

put wreaths on your mother's birthplace. The best I can
do is buy you a plain oak cross that will be protected
by a metal box sunk into the hillside of headstones.

The inscription will be: *PAULA HITLER: 1896-1960.*
Like a poppy, your brother must have been the flower
of a dark seed. Your memories are a tapeworm that

will die with you, and you should not try to forgive what
should never be forgiven. You are God's child. Believe
the promise in rain: there is something new on the way.

Assignment for Week Four: Poem about Another Person

Winter hardens New Haven. Wind that chips at sleeves
and pockets makes men like Tony, who croon syllables to
muscatel then piss behind stairways on Howe Street, sad

to have hands. There were years when Tony had enough
to rent a room at the Taft Hotel. Spring days, he would lean
out of his window in a sleeveless undershirt. Now, he's lucky

if he gets to sleep at Viva Zapata on rice bags the cooks store
in piles near a furnace to keep them dry. Most days, Tony
has his own stool at the bar in Rudy's on the corner of Elm

and Howe. The bartender, Marty, lets him use the john
with enough light to read handwriting of a twenty-year-old
Yalie who doesn't care enough to dot the *i* or cross the *t*.

I'm a regular and from the state school across town. It's okay
if I buy Tony's story for my poem by picking up his tab
for Jack Daniels and Sam Adams he normally can't afford.

Tactful, I make mental notes as I ask, *What makes you drink
so hard, drink shots and beer at nine in the morning?* Tony
mumbles about Champion Auto, how he operated two bays,

two at one time. Listening, a girl with a bulldog on her hat
drinks coffee, leans back on a wall plastered with Whaler's
banners, Raven's baseballs, football photos taken at the Bowl.

To show her what I know, how clever I can be, I try to quote
Drink? or think? better drink. Charles Bukowski is dead,
and there's a spot I can fill. No need for me to live the lines.

For the price of another round, I can gather authentic detail,
get Tony to talk about how he tried to end World War II
by cutting his wrists, but bleeding was too slow. Each shot

of whiskey brings him closer to the bar, face fallen forward.
Some days he cuts his forehead, but the bouncer lets him sit
and drink beer as long as he's good for the business at Rudy's.

The owners, Michael and Hank, have left orders about what
to do if Tony starts to shake his fist and mutter, *You goddamn
Yalie! I operated two bays at one time, two bays at one time.*

KYRIE ELEISON

For William Slone Coffin

No Beethoven cracking gates of heaven,
you stand in Battell Chapel, stained glass
windows darkening to late afternoon. Plants
in Yale's Old Campus are only Swiss chard,
the rest withered shadows from *Job*.
Like fingernails on a chalkboard, sirens
in B flat interrupt this December solstice.
Where are the halcyon days? You've counted
seven days in a row of bad weather. Pacing
to forestall thought of seven more, you resume
practicing *Jesu Christi*, your entry as the baritone
for the quartet in Verdi's *Requiem*. Throat muscles
atrophy: *Jesu Christi, Jesu Christi*. You need
daffodils, not winter weeds disappearing to gray.

YET WE WERE WRONG, TERRIBLY WRONG.

—Robert S. McNamara
Secretary of Defense, 1961-1968

Dressed in a black three-piece suit with a roll of toilet paper
    in one hand and a Bible in the other, your brother starts
at the corner of Wooster Square Park on Chapel Street
    then parades until he spots an elm that suits him. Before

spending two years in Vietnam, he would walk up State Street
    to the front window of the drugstore and stand
by Joseph Rosenthal's A.P. photograph of an American flag
    being raised on Mt. Suribachi at the top of Iwo Jima.

In WWII, when the Fifth Marine Division made it to the summit
    after four days of battle, your father was one of six men
who raised the flag. He died within days. It was late February,
    early March of 1945. There were banners in the windows

with stars on them. Blue meant someone from that house
    was in the service, and a gold star meant someone had died.
Your grandmother's house had three stars, two blue, one gold.
    Then another turned to gold. Your brother still has the letters

written by your father about the firefights: Marines would hold
    weapons over a ridge, exposing only hands and upper arms
to return fire. Letters were filled with Ira Hayes, a Pima Indian
    who also raised the flag but who survived to die of alcohol.

Hayes would pop up to shoot, flop back down to reload. During
    one mortar attack, he walked off to relieve himself.
Six thousand, two hundred died on Iwo Jima in shallow gulches,
    from snipers, shells being lobbed. Hayes was the soldier

your brother wanted to be when he enlisted and asked to be
    shipped to Da Nang. There were no flags to raise, no pictures
in *The New Haven Register*, no stars in windows. Not a battle
    statistic like your father, your brother is unable to drown

himself in shots and beers like Hayes. He will take nothing
    from the living but cannot stop what the dead drain
out of him. Shouting at the elm tree about bodies splitting
    apart, your brother hurls the roll of paper high into air.

Is each layer a beginning, wiping out years in Vietnam that are
    like ice on the window spreading into a jungle of ferns
or waiting fingers? Streaming like a rocket unrolling all the way
    to heaven, the tissue always misses the branches and piles

in the street. Shrugging it off, your brother goes back home
    to your mother who never complains about the mess,
but worries over the extravagance of it, the waste of good paper.
    Your cousin Joyce stuffed cotton in her cheeks to fill them

out, but she didn't throw it away. Dried over night, the balls were
    used again and again. The toilet paper is useless, melting
into the street like years your brother spent waiting out the dark,
    knowing every stumbling place his hand might touch down

on a face. Eyes were always open, darker than veined coca
    leaves or concentrated like pools of light in silk from Hanoi.
Sucked back, your brother confronts the eyes and your father,
    the look on his face, as he braces to raise the flag, making

shoulders ache with the permanence of it. No Joseph Rosenthal
    photograph of your brother in the drugstore, no red, white,
and blue, only black lining to a wall of eyes that will never close,
    that will never disappear, that words of remorse cannot erase.

No Need to Buy *The New York Times*

Catch the week's massacre in Darfur on Saturday and Sunday
scrubbing white alabaster of Beinecke Library, its walls a shield
for William Blake's *Songs of Innocence and of Experience*

with his *tyger* and *lamb* you'll never get an afternoon off to see.
But Yale is generous, lets you take fifteen minutes for coffee
and a cigarette after punching the clock before you scour spirals

of red, blue, and black with Top Job and turpentine. 11,000 slabs
are perfect canvas for Connecticut's night priests who spray
with aerosol cans. You are grateful to them for your steady job.

The death toll, this week Iraq, never stops. Today, it's Al Aksa
Brigades' suicide bombings in Baghdad or Zarqawi televising
hostage beheadings. Tomorrow, Al Qaeda, Osama bin Laden,

Chechnya, or genocide in Sudan. Maybe James Jones dreamed
up the title *From Here to Eternity* watching you go to work
each day past Naples Pizza. It's a sure bet the mayor won't erect

a bronze statue by Seward Johnson of you on the green: a man
thickened by age squatting in a Red Sox's cap. But, hey, you're
paid by the hour to clean, keep New Haven's workdays spotless.

Why should you care? Bless politicians who fuel protests. Pray
Yalies keep dripping graffiti on white alabaster. Using Brillo pads
on the concrete sidewalks is harder on your arms and knees.

ACTION NEWS, CHANNEL EIGHT

It's not the woman crying, her dead son, the unfenced
      tracks, or the train and driver that we talk about.
            It's the camera, the photographer who keeps

filming, zooming in for a close up of her face while
      a policeman holds the mother back right as she learns
            who is dead. Clouds pack the sky, a blue heron

slips while spearing a fish, and we laugh so hard, we let
      our back issues of *POETRY* drop. Our eyes close,
            last night's six o'clock news, twisted lips intrude.

In a day or two, when we pause, we probably won't think
      of that mouth, of the mother in New Haven with
            no son, no morning bacon to fry for him to smell.

You Had the Choice, Martha

as you clocked second month: gut, firm
flat dinner plate or inflated rubber glove.
Despite the doctor's warning, you did not
have your son sucked out, preserved in saline
to let the technicians sample fetal bone.
Like a suitcase, you lugged your stomach,
elastic as Siamese skin upholstering two bodies.

Blasphemy of love you cannot now abort:
Lesch-Nyan. One in one hundred million,
but when it's yours, a statistic isn't a number
but a child. Your heart burns at words that bother
him so, whispered from that irreplaceable face.
You do not love Robby less for his caged heart
or because he must always be lifted to the van,
hands tied so he will not gouge out his eyes,
teeth pulled to stop gnawing at arms. Scars
are the letters you must keep him from learning,
knowing he is taught nothing by the pain,
but that it feeds a need that can never be filled.

Spoon him your dreams, even though your son,
the trickster, spits them back on the kitchen tile.
Slip, slide, skate through. Lift your arms, an angel
in flight in spite of what you do that is so human:
buying the blue bicycle, propping it by the bed
in Robby's room, building a ramp that you know
he will never pump, coast, or brake, flinging gravel.

Sylvia Plath Should Have Planted a Garden

In the Strawbery Banke Museum's garden, lemon day lilies
open their lips as if to speak to me. Perhaps they are waiting
to be fed by Puritans who brought them to New Hampshire
and planted roads leading to Portsmouth. Clumps were dug
and transplanted by thrifty New Englanders. Orange field lilies,
impossible to erase like dandelion roots, also bank interstates
in July, but they are way too common to invade this exotic

collection, laid out as if quilted and edged into blocks
of English herbs. L-shaped around the garden, the house
was built by a sea captain. About to climb the steps
to a widow's walk that crowns the museum, the lure
of an opium poppy's round pod, grayish green leaves,
white and purple flowers draws me outside. Volunteers
have yanked out chickweed, and already punk with heads

of seed, bull thistle has been carted off for the compost.
I can almost see the captain returning after two years
at sea: hands on hips, elbows bent outward, arms akimbo
like lamb's quarters. His wife's shoulders might have been
bare as iris tubers, her desire for him strong enough to push
through winter into spring in spite of shovel after shovel
of dirt she had lifted in the garden. Did she count out black

poppy seeds to stop the pain of giving birth unattended?
Would she have known to collect yellow brown juice
from unripe capsules to mix an opiate to stop time, thought
of suffocating then burying a child born too many months
after her husband set sail? She would have had no woman,

no doctor to befriend her, to give alkaloids of morphine,
codeine, or papaverine that would produce sleep or to perform

an abortion at night so none of the neighbors would witness
the coming, the going, the record of a passion that should
have been controlled. Knowing I've let my mind get away
from me again, I go to the museum shop to learn if the captain
brought poppy seeds from China. Selling note cards, a woman
who's even older than me sits in a stiff lilac dress. I hadn't
smelled starch since I was little: the steam and my mother

testing the hot iron with her spittled finger, then the hiss
that always startled both of us. Smell of cotton, evanescent
as everything we can't hold onto, pulls at my body, reminds
me of games I was good at playing: Statues, Red Light,
Jailhouse. I would freeze, invisible, not a finger moving,
an eye blinking, like the captain's wife, clever enough
not to get caught. *May I help you?* jerks me back. I ask

to buy poppy seeds or gather them from the garden. That's
illegal. Pulling a sweater over her name tag, the woman says
she'll send me some from her sister's garden, even though it
will mean breaking the law. No return address, an envelope
arrives; I plant seeds, careful to follow directions, then store
the rest in an unmarked jar. However small, these illicit acts
between women will flower, bind us together, keep us alive.

METAMORPHOSES

I. REVISING THE CANON: A STAG PARTY

Too much light to read. At ease, Actaeon and his men
dripped in blood they hunted hot, burning. Inlet shade,

Diana bathed with Crocale and Hephele, arms unsheathed.
Only the sea was fertile, no other fluids caressing. Odor

of shellfish, open mussels, the gills of a fish and its fins
brushed their breasts, sweet as a tongue flicking nipples.

Hollowed by the women's heels, holes foamed as calves
were pushed apart. Receding waves sucked, melted

their buttocks that skinned rhythms on sand never tracked
by any man. Each lathering the other—knees, shoulders,

navels, and backs—fingers snaked, probed, then spread lips
to water, wet, warm as a woman's mouth. Brown strands

of unbound hair wove into seaweed wrapping thighs. No
thrust, only licking then curling. Nothing hard until Hephele

glanced at Actaeon, protruding above them. Diana reddened,
resentful of this pleasure cheaply gained. Having no weapon,

she let words fly: *Boast if you can that you have seen Diana
naked.* This chance but crucial junction shocked marrow

in his bones. As inner and outer self merged, horns grew.
Words froze like lard in his throat at the baying of Harpy

and Tigress, independent bitches who picked out hounds
they would let mount them to service the pack. Air filled

with teeth; Actaeon moaned as the dogs snarled. Now, he
was the one ripped open, pressed down, legs apart with no

escape. One bitch stripped his flank; another tore at his head.
Some thought Diana merciless; others praised her sentence.

II. DAPHNE AND APOLLO

Daphne was another independent love and marriage
hating young huntress and no wonder. Women one
after the other had either aborted, lost their names,
or gassed themselves in the long procession. The most
Daphne might expect was to drag from state to state
packing, unpacking, papering bathroom walls in tigers.
She wrote couplets, sang them to every man she met:

If men were golden rods growing,
women would get scythes for mowing.

If men were trout in water clear,
smart women would grab a sharp spear.

If men like deer on hills did run,
women would learn to shoot a gun.

A hound flushing a rabbit, Apollo ran for game, Daphne
safety. Worn out, a victim to long flight, her limbs grew
numb, rooted to the ground. Hair pruned, she kissed
Apollo with wooden lips and wreathed his head, a laurel.

III. *New Haven Register's Symphony Supplement:*
"Mrs. Jove Models Latest Fur"

Io tightened sheets stretched through her thighs
as oak limbs, or what she hoped were branches
and not tips of horns, scraped her window. Only
leaves breathed as Jove hoofed the screen, climbed

through. No sound from Io as Jove entered her,
pausing only for a final contraction that was like a jet
of milk ringing into a pail. White, shiny as a heifer,
Io became his bride, wreathed in diamonds set in

gold, not a brass nose ring like a common cow.
She was licensed and then recorded under Jove.
Chain linked in a pasture, beleaguered by gadflies,
milk cows can grow too old to freshen. Shopping

for cruise wear, Io drove her Range Rover from Saks
to Lord & Taylor's, then Bloomingdale's. No Wal-Mart
or Marshall's for Jove's wife. Io volunteered, played
tennis, did speed training with a personal trainer, got

a pedicure every day. Getting through meals of pasta,
sauce on the side, Prozac didn't silence the lowing
filling her throat. Fingering dust the new maid had left
on a piano, she engraved an *I* and *O*, wiped them clean.

IV. SCIENTIFIC KNIVES ARE SHARP, NOT MYTHICAL

When Iphis forced her way from womb to day,
Telethusa could picture her new daughter
with breasts rising into small mounds. Ligdus

had fathered Iphis saying, *If it should be a girl,*
throttle her, drown her like a cat. Saving strength
in her hands to knead bread, Telethusa told Ligdus

he had a son. After thirteen years of balancing
on the tightrope of her mother's lie, Iphis trembled
when she was betrothed to Ianthe, knew that

the girl would want a bridegroom not another bride.
Passing as a boy, she had studied biology. Reassured
by classroom rote, Iphis chose a surgeon who could

spout facts to be her god. Trans-sexual operations
were an anatomy lesson in pink and blue paint,
but not a slight procedure: breasts flattened, nipples

remained, labia sewn shut, lumps and a sausage roll
of flesh added. Prick the skin and hormones passed.
Up through half light to day, an empty elevator

clanged its doors, a bare stretcher trembled. No
one sang her song, held rattles or torches. Iphis
had three legs at last and rising on two of them,

made way to a toilet where mortal coils distilled
a drop. Proud, the doctor unwrapped his wedding
gift for Ianthe. Finally, Iphis was his father's son.

V. Pygmalion and Galatea

One man, Pygmalion, had seen shameful women
leading lives as surgeons slicing male genitals
or perfecting a uterus that snapped in and out.
He was shocked at their vices: females cursed,

kept their own names, gave birth alone to children,
did not scrub toilets. Pygmalion knew that nature
had given women wombs and breasts as armor
for motherhood, no more. He lived alone, placed

no one in his bed until he found a girl like a piece
of unchiseled marble. Skilled as Pygmalion was
in the art of concealing art, he molded carefully
and named her, Galatea. Loving ways he could play

with his workmanship, his doll, he tucked Galatea
in bed at night, but not before spreading her legs.
Mounted like a hobbyhorse, she made no sound,
not even *MaMa* or *DaDa*. Even marble grows softer

under the heat of hands. Galatea started to change
at Pygmalion's touch: nipples would rise, veins
throbbed under his thumb, her breath quickened
almost as if a goddess had intervened. In a rainbow

after a storm, colors blend. Even though the eye
cannot detect a line, the arcs are altogether different.
Pygmalion could not define the boundary Galatea
had crossed, but she was not humble in his presence.

Grafted, twigs knit and mature. Galatea was filled
with blooms, an apple tree with promise. Refusing
this harvest, Pygmalion's passion waned as frost does
dissolving over crocus on an early spring morning.

VI. Arethusa Speaks to Alpheus as He Pursues Her

You offer your shaft as something I could use.
　　The shape is handsome and unmarked as a new
　　mushroom, I will admit. Responsive, intelligent,
you say. I could teach it to perform, move about

upon command, come and fetch me long strings
　　of lapis, azure beaded by gold. Tented on your pole,
　　my labia could fold, take your shape, rise moist
as pliable canvas, and fill like a sail on the mast

of a ship. Placing my mouth around it, I would say
　　only that like the sea, your staff lacks perfume,
　　tastes of salt. There must be some talent to raise
it high above the ordinary. Can it sing like Pavarotti?

Though the shape is very suggestive, I cannot
　　find a use for it, even to stir soups or pen poems,
　　but I will keep my left hand in your pants pocket
for one week, if I must, in order to learn your ebb

and flow. Now your cock seems tame enough
　　while I stroke it, limp as a flounder, slightly damp.
　　Good God! It moves. Who trained it to live erect
and hard without air, without warmth or a home?

Still, it continues, sturdy as a prickly pear cactus.
　　Will it bloom for only one night like the cereus?
　　I think I should tell you that I have two deft hands,
plenty for my need. You might take their place.

I ask only that you never climb into bed, slide under
　　covers, and grab my genitals like a blind limb
　　thrusting toward heat. You should begin at the top
of my throat on my lips that are treacherous. Solitude

has taught me how to shape and then speak empty
   promises to other men. Become a stream, make
   your way far under bushes, dive deep in my tunnel,
mingle your water with mine. Let the fountain spray!

VII. Brueghel's *Icarus*: An Old Husband's Tale

> *how it takes place / While someone else is eating*
> —W. H. Auden

Daedalus was not a man, Icarus no boy. That's a myth.
Without a husband to bind her, Daedalus turned nature
inside out, taught her daughter to fly from earth; after all,

men couldn't fence air. Feathering Icarus in the sequence
of a pan pipe rising, Daedalus twined quills and molded two
sets of wings sealed in icing of white wax, stiff as bridal lace.

Daedalus hovered, warning: *Keep mid-way; water weighs
and sun burns. Always follow me.* Icarus rose or was pulled
up, casting her shadow on a ploughman, head lifted from

his rut, who grumbled, *A woman's place is in the home.*
The mother tried to lift arms higher to buffer her daughter,
but blue enveloped Icarus who cried, *Let's fly all the way*

to Trinacria! Knowing Samos was north and Calymne east,
Icarus ignored earth's warning being traced out for her
by the sharded coast of Crete. Filial duty cannot blot desire

like the moon eclipsing sun. Perhaps there was a brilliance
gleaming in Icarus's green eyes that flashed and mercifully
blocked the sight for Daedalus: her only child encircling

wings, writhing like a corn snake carried aloft by a hawk.
Imagine the girl, her mother's support failing, aerial lift
and impulse spent. Dripping into sea, only white wax

hissed, floating as islands do. Daedalus did not fly again.
Unused, feathers yellowed. Wax stiffened in her wings
that stretched out more like a shroud than a swan in flight.

For the Friend I Cannot Replace

Am Braighe was what we could not reach. Gibberish
I called it, but in Gaelic, you told me, it was higher ground

sought by your people from the Lochaber district
of the Highlands. The Cabot Strait below us, we crossed

hills that seemed to brood over lakes misted in like those
your great-grandfather had to leave in Scotland for this land

in Nova Scotia. It was 1842; he was cleared from his farm
by a landlord who earned more money shearing herds

of sheep than collecting rent. Baddeck, Big Harbour,
your father was already asleep when you came to say

goodbye, when you came to say the rehearsed *I love you*
to him, words I struggled to help you breathe out

with each step of the Cape Breton hill. Moored in the bay,
you could not say the words even to me. You leaned

to hear what your father could not say, what he would
never say: *Come back.* There was the letter he did not write

telling you about the day your mother died. As if asleep,
the tumor was behind her closed eyes, like a penny she hid

in birthday cakes iced for you. I could have shown you
the x-ray of a tumor taken from my head, but I could not

repeat your mother's last words. After her death, there
were days of silence when I wanted to talk to you. Speak,

I would say. All or nothing but not this. It was crazy
when you were here, Wendy. You'd leave after lunch.

I'd fall asleep in the middle of the afternoon, waking
only when my sons came home from soccer practice

for take-out egg rolls and lo-mein. Where did words
you would not say go? Words I did not say have stayed.

Some days, I can not stop myself from going downtown,
sitting in New Haven Terminal to listen for a train I dream

you on. A ticket agent, one boot propped on a counter,
watches me as I wait for your voice, the words you have

not said. I know the train has arrived, people crowd
by me—but not you. The blackboard schedule is erased.

5

Last Light

What to Do about Sharks

1.   If a hammerhead or a great white makes
waves during your workshop or poetry reading,
don't flap your elbows or slap at it with rolled
manuscripts. Sharks thrive on visual stimulation.

2.   Blow out candles. Ease away from the podium,
and wait at least ten minutes before going
for a light switch. Join hands to keep karma
with the other poets. It's okay to recite
poems you memorized in fifth grade,
Joyce Kilmer, in desperation, even Longfellow.

3.   Rule of thumb: it's a shark not a dolphin
if it is slamming about the room, hugging,
blowing air kisses. Performers, sharks
are almost all instinct and no brain. Without
sense of occasion, they'll crash any gig,
underwater or not, from Madagascar to Malibu.

4.   Being eyed by a shark can be exasperating,
but don't rush or shift from foot to foot
to induce motion sickness. Sharks are immune.
They are, however, dyslexic. Flash cover quotes,
prize-winning poems directly in front of both eyes.
Better yet—stop reading. Pull your new hardback
from a knapsack, and if the shark noses you
with repeated sharp jabs, hit it on the snout.

5.   If all else fails, sharks have a keen sense
of hearing. Sing *The Battle Hymn of the Republic*
at the top of your lungs. Sharks have short
attention spans, get bored, leave if there is
no open mike. So, swing into another verse:
Glory! Glory! Hallelujah! His truth is marching on.

NO CREEL LIMIT

The wind must have forgotten. It's August.
    There's that Long Island chop;
        fish are everywhere. Snappers are

in, roiling scalloped waves as shiners leap
    into silver fireworks, cascading
        onto the shore. Whip the boat

to full throttle! No putt, putt or hanging over
    the stern to drift, like we did casting in
        Vermont ponds, black with pines.

I want wake, spreading to angel wings.
    There must be sound, splashing,
        slapping, more than a line arcing,

more than the hiss of a swan. Don't relive
    last week with no wind to shunt
        away humidity, dilute mugginess,

or ruffle the skin. This spot is guaranteed.
    Throw in bait, it will be wasted like
        quarters dropped in St. Barnabas's

collection plate. Solid as words filling page
    after page, blues will hook themselves
        and jump right up into our boat

if we don't catch them. We may have been
    searching for answers, for fish
        that were not around, but today

they are on the surface, floating almost into air
for gulls to snatch without calling,
without diving, without getting wet.

CHUM

Nor need you mind the serial ordeal
—Robert Frost

1. I fish when three sons and a husband are not enough.

A fan unfolding, water bands the cove signaling the first sign
of spring in Long Island Sound: winter flounder. The key
word to learn is chum, a mixture of clams, mussels, and fish
parts allowed to thaw in a bag as it drifts in the current.
The manual reads drop a sandworm and you'll see flounder.
If that doesn't work, I score with plugs like Red Fin, Bomber,
and buck tails by the mouth of Connecticut River and Watch Hill.

2. I fish because I don't want summer to end.

Chum can be abandoned since summer flounder called fluke
like a clean sandy bottom. Bigger than winter flounder, they
have teeth, feed on small fish but will hit a variety of bait. I
catch fluke in the red-hot Norwalk Islands on live snappers or
herring or squid strips. Reciting verse helps to fill silence of
dry spells: *if you're lost enough to find yourself / By now, pull
in your ladder road behind you / And put a sign up CLOSED.*

3. I fish to find what is missing, the friend I don't have to call.

Poetry won't wilt the memory: me, standing behind a podium
after the fiction reading, counting money collected for *Folio*
while everyone else has gone out to drink at the Cape Codder.
Driving home, I make up reasons why I'm never asked: I don't
know Felix the Cat is acid or have suns tattooed on a forearm;
I am too fat, too old, too much the mother. I try to wash off
loneliness the next day but it stays, a stain that won't soak out.

4. I fish since the search never ends for keys, a chum, love.

I cannot learn how to forget, tire of carrying the whole weight
of memory like an audience: mother, father, sisters, three sons.
Yet, like an atom, I seek company. Surely, heaven is stripped
of need for talk, for touch. Even when I know summer is gone,
fish on Morgan Point's bottom have migrated to deep water off
shore, I fish, keeping lures that worked before, letting chum drift
just in case for the flounder I can't see that might still be there.

Woman's Guide to Salt Water Fishing

Chapter I. Tarpon: The Wildest One

They are any woman's fish. No need for sleek cabin cruisers, heavy tackle, deep water, because the tarpon's a light tackle fish; catch one from a skiff or an outboard runabout. Difficult to label, the tarpon has many names: the silver king or *savanilla,* in Louisiana the *grande ecaille,* and in Latin America the *sabalo.* The tarpon loves to explore mangrove swamps and lagoons. If you are looking for more than a good time, keep in mind that he goes to shallow rivers in the spring to spawn, but if you want to fish just for the kicks, this crazy fish will bat a plug into the air, slash at it several times. After all, it's the aerial acrobatics you should be after. Feeling the hook, the wild one goes completely berserk and can hurl himself as much as ten feet out of the water to break loose. Keep your barbs, like your nails, needle sharp. Change your lines frequently and test them before fishing to be sure there are no weak spots. Wear sunglasses; never make unnecessary noise. Once a tarpon is nervous, he's very hard to tease into striking. There is no better time to try for a tarpon than a warm sultry summer night when wet air thickens like his deep body with its compressed flanks and those large, powerful fins. Pay particular attention to the last ray of the dorsal, which is distinctively elongated and burnished to silver. Size does matter.

Chapter II. Snook: The Merry-Go-Round Fish

Unlike the tarpon, the snook isn't much of an aerialist, goes in for a brief wallowing on the surface. It's lucky for the snook that beauty is in the eye of the beholder, because his head is very flat with a strong protruding lower jaw. Fortunately, he has no teeth just bristles along the jaw rim and tongue, and this makes him suitable for certain activities you may enjoy. Go for the gold, for the jumbo, the biggest snook of all, who pours through passes at Caxambas, Big and Little March Island. Fish during the spring tide, the tag end of May when the royal poinciana start to bloom in Marco Island, halfway between Everglades City and Naples. Florida's Shark River country is also a great snook hot spot. A woman's dream come true, young or old, a snook can be ridiculously easy to fool. Plugs like the Pflueger Pal-O-Mine have the typical wiggle that snook seem to grab. There's no need to dig for live bait, feather or nylon jigs will do, but snook do love shrimp and crabs, which make them ideal for a happy hour or two. Strong, fairly fast, lively but low jumpers, they are terrific laid on the table. A snook either doesn't understand or won't play by rules causing other women to veer clear out of formation. The minute a good snook strikes, it is sheer bedlam. Everyone will have to cut lines or buy new ones unless you can agree to troll in a circle, follow an orderly pattern, and get a pecking order.

CHAPTER III. THE SAILFISH: THE GLADIATOR

Roaming in the open sea, the sailfish is distinguished by his long slender spearlike nose. His tail is symmetrical and deeply forked. Most exciting of all are his pecs, which are bigger and longer than any other billfish. Beautiful and metallic, it isn't until a sailfish is startled, excited, or injured that he becomes really vivid. Whole waves of color, purple to blue, flash through his body. Like Harley motorcycle packs, sailfish travel in small groups, and it should be a warning to any woman who sees them when they ball a school of small fish in one spot. While one sailfish knifes and probes the smaller fish with his bill, the others circle and jump wildly into air in a strange and frenzied manner. At another time, the sailfish will strike the instant he sights bait, lashing out with his bill. Still another will follow, stalking behind like a hyena following a stricken antelope. Mounting, the suspense is almost impossible to stand. The sailfish wants bait that appears to be alive with no mind of its own. Be sure to take the backbone out so the baitfish becomes limp but still can give a genuine live performance as it bounces across the surface. When a sailfish leaps and greyhounds across the ocean's surface, don't confuse him with the marlin who sometimes tail-walks almost a hundred feet or more. Hold out for that spear, tail, and pecs. Here's a final word of warning: a sailfish can do strange things to otherwise normal women once he is hooked.

Chapter IV. Barracuda

Of course, he's a killer but so is every other male that swims. A barracuda is only more efficient, and unlike the sailfish, he does not hunt in packs. Like the tarpon, he can be taken by a woman of any age from a rowboat or from a bridge. Cudas can be found in mangrove channels or on open weedy flats, while cruising over coral reefs or on the edge of ocean currents. In water with dark bars, he's hard to spot. Formidable looking with a weird grin, the barracuda is unusually curious, likes to swim up very close and stay there in order to watch everything that goes on. Most trophy specimens are taken on live or cut bait. Chumming, incidentally, is another technique to attract him. A word to the wise: the young barracuda is the most willing of strikers. The bait can be alive or artificial, floating or sinking. He will usually wallop bait as soon as he sees it, but once a barracuda becomes an adult, he looks mighty carefully at brightly colored artificial lures, and then he can seldom be fooled by the plastic he smells, even though platinum American Express credit cards have been known to lure him.

Trespassers at Morgan Point

Cautious as a stag leading does into a clearing, two fishermen
look at the house, just checking. As if crossing a lawn they had

newly seeded, their steps are shortened, rods held low. Heading
for low tide, the black rocks, one holds his son's hand, knowing

full well the Zodiac is beached above high water on pink granite.
Not trying to claim they are lost, confused, or sorry when I point

to *Private Property*, it's anger for me simmering in their throats
that idles like an outboard motor. A United jet taking off from

Tweed New Haven censors *bitch*. No Roger Tory Peterson,
neither of them will teach the boy to tell a white heron from

a snowy egret by an egret's black bill, black legs, and yellow feet.
Busy popping caps off Rolling Rock, the father doesn't point

to another egret shuffling feet about in order to stir up shiners,
a habit white herons don't have. Calling a cormorant *crow* even

when it spreads wings like an eagle, he teaches his son to break
Skyy vodka bottles for blue sea glass. We are all trespassers

of one sort or another, but that does it! I dial the East Haven
police and demand protection. When their red lights flash, I gloat

while snapper after snapper jumps as if drawn by a magnet into
the cove. Badge or no badge, I know these fishermen will be

back, the boy carrying beer. On good days, or bad, if a rip
feathers the Sound, it will be a sign to them, irrepressible as tide.

Soon, soon

my son would whisper as I pictured netting dark,
    not our bait darting into tide pool moss.
        Twilight was best with shadows

crossing and uncrossing like legs of cheerleaders
    seated on bleachers at a home game.
        Brushing sand lice from my knees

and thighs, I'd lecture to myself, *There is a limit.*
    Our insurance against lures, Matthew scooped
        kellys into a pickle jar, but fearing

for his thumb I hooked them onto his rod. I turned
    away when the bluefish struck, knowing
        what I would have to do, that my son

was still too young to handle a knife. My fingers
    wrestling its insides, guts over my wrist,
        I was grateful no sun gleamed in

the fish's eyes. Rubbing my index finger's knuckle
    under my nose, a habit I couldn't break,
        I would inhale the smell for days.

Like squid left to dry that curl and stick to the deck,
    scales of the fish I cleaned fell to silver
        grass. Staying put through winter,

washed by spring rain, scales glittered on asphalt,
    rolled as if on the bluefish's flesh leaping off
        the hook to forgive, to resurrect my hands.

Last Light

Pack up your gear, head for The Quinney Quencher
    if you haven't speared a sturgeon ice fishing
      on Lake Winnebago. Chug the house specialty,
a beer with a minnow in it. Required: a dark shack,

one big hole, and the willingness to stare for hours.
    You must let go of all the adjectives you've
      been saving for *boring*. Describe looking
up your chimney waiting for a duck to fly over or

your father in Joshua Tree living seventeen years
    watching for a nolina in his side yard to
      bloom. Desert people know how to wait
for magic, for a flower that is not minor, that is not

common. Some years, hillsides of nolinas send up
    spikes as big as a leg. When the bud unfolds,
      it's the size of a family Christmas tree like
discarded evergreens used to mark roads plowed

by Otter Street Fishing Club into grids crisscrossing
    Lake Winnebago. Twenty inches of frozen water
      and 3,779 shanties will give you faith needed
to walk on ice lugging black paint for inside walls

of your shanty. Sturgeon avoid light. No windows,
    sun penetrating ice will supply illumination,
      a yellow-green glow from a hole big as a kitchen
table that you cut in ice. Waiting, hum the theme

from Beethoven's last piano sonata, the one where
    you imagine him looking through the bright
    entry of the world into the dark. It's okay to sing
but illegal to drop bait for a sturgeon. Sit over the hole,

jiggle decoys and wait for the fish's natural curiosity
    to surface. For lures, you can carve a wooden
    walleye, weight it with lead or with your brother's
plastic pipe dripping round mirrors and plastic figures

of Sesame Street's Miss Piggy and Cookie Monster.
    Willing to experiment? Dangle an agitator
    out of a Maytag washing machine, Styrofoam
coffee cup, or even a bowling ball painted green with

pink spots like Brett Olson who has speared fifteen
    sturgeon, his quota of one a year, since he
    turned fourteen. Brett swears his catch all
came in so fast, they headed the bowling ball and

rolled over. If you do sight a sturgeon, drop the spear
    hanging from the ceiling, don't throw it.
    Spear fishing is about trusting your eight-foot
twenty-pound shaft. Attached to fifty feet of nylon

rope, its tips should hang under the surface, disengage
    so your dinner can't pull away. Don't become
    discouraged. Like the bloom of the nolina,
the sturgeon is worth the wait. Syd Groeschl has tried

for fifty years; Tom Springborn has had no luck for
    nineteen. Both know their prize must be right there
    beneath them. Arms ache from stretching, from hoping
to pull out that five feet and a hundred pounds of fish.

It is the chance to prepare one themselves, taste smoke
from their own wood that keeps Syd and Tom
crossing Wisconsin ice each winter—that and having
their picture taken while weighing in for the cover story

in *USA Today*. Camera shy, for you the appeal is that
the sturgeon is so old it's been swimming in silence,
tireless as a glacier, for 150 to 200 million years
through dinosaurs, wilderness, and other predators.

Resting under your feet, it offers a way to absorb part
of your past and frees you from having to visit
mounted skeletons in the Smithsonian. Hooded
in bone, lessons about survival are trapped by a world

of coded cells in this fish that has swallowed the flesh
of centuries. Learning patience from your father,
you have seen the nolina bloom. It is enough for
you that, in the darkness below, your dream is waiting.

⊿ ACKNOWLEDGMENTS ⊾

Grateful acknowledgment is made to the editors of the journals in which these poems, often in earlier versions, first appeared: the *American Scholar, Another Chicago Magazine, Arkansas Review,* the *Centennial Review,* the *Chattahoochee Review, Chachalaca Poetry Review,* the *Christian Science Monitor, Confrontation, Curious Rooms,* the *Evansville Review,* the *Florida Review, Flyway, Footwork, Fugue, Georgetown Review, Hamline Journal, Hayden's Ferry Review, Heliotrope: A Journal of Poetry, The Journal, Kalliope, The Ledge, Louisiana Literature,* the *Lowell Pearl, Many Mountains Moving,* the *Nebraska Review, Negative Capability, New York Quarterly, Painted Bride Quarterly, Paterson Literary Review, Pearl, Piedmont Literary Review, Pleiades, Poets On, Quarterly West, Red Rock Review, River Styx Magazine, Rockhurst Review, Sheila-Na-Gig, Slant,* the *Spoon River Poetry Review, So to Speak, Synaesthesia, Tampa Review,* the *Vanderbilt Review, Voices West, War, Literature & the Arts, Whiskey Island Magazine,* the *Wisconsin Review, Yarrow, Yawp Magazine,* and *Yemassee.*

✑ ABOUT THE AUTHOR ✑

Connecticut State University Distinguished Professor at Southern Connecticut State University and Editor of *Connecticut Review*, Vivian Shipley has published eleven books of poetry. *Gleanings: Old Poems, New Poems* won the 2004 Paterson Award for Sustained Literary Achievement, and *When There Is No Shore* won the 2003 Connecticut Book Prize for Poetry from Library of Congress's Center for the Book. Other poetry awards include the Lucille Medwick Prize from the Poetry Society of America, the Robert Frost Foundation Poetry Prize, the Ann Stanford Poetry Prize from the University of Southern California, the Julia Peterkin Prize from Converse College, the Marble Faun Poetry Prize from the William Faulkner Society, the Daniel Varoujan Prize from the New England Poetry Club, the Hart Crane Prize from Kent State University and a Connecticut Commission on the Arts grant. Vivian Shipley lives in North Haven, Connecticut with her husband, Ed Harris.